P9-DXI-643

# Just 5 Things

Rachel Lane

# Just 5 Things

Easy Gourmet Cooking with Just a Handful of Ingredients

THE READER'S DIGEST ASSOCIATION, INC.
PLEASANTVILLE, NEW YORK / MONTREAL / LONDON / SYDNEY

A READER'S DIGEST BOOK
This edition published by the Reader's Digest Association by arrangement with McRae Books Srl


Desserts
was created and produced by McRae Books Srl
Via del Salviatino, 1 – 50016 Fiesole, Florence, Italy
info@mcraebooks.com
www.mcraebooks.com
Publishers: Anne McRae, Marco Nardi

FOR MCRAE BOOKS
Project Director Anne McRae
Art Director Marco Nardi
Photography Brent Parker Jones
Photographic Art Direction Neil Hargreaves
Texts Rachel Lane, Carla Bardi, Ting Morris
Food Styling Lee Blaylock, Neil Hargreaves
Layouts Aurora Granata
Pre-press Filippo Delle Monache

FOR READER'S DIGEST
U.S. Project Editor: Andrea Chesman
Project Designer: Jen Tokarski
Executive Editor, Trade Publishing: Dolores York
Director, Trade Publishing: Rosanne McManus
Vice President & Publisher, Trade Publishing: Harold Clarke

ISBN 978-0-7621-0980-7

Printed in China

The level of difficulty for each recipe is given on a scale from 1 (easy) to 3 (complicated).

# CONTENTS

# INTRODUCTION



Cooking with just a handful of ingredients will not only save you time and money but will also let you rediscover the natural, basic flavors of foods. You will learn how to combine them so that they subtly complement each other without creating an overload of contradictory tastes and aromas. By using a contained ingredient palette, these recipes concentrate on classic taste combinations, such as pasta, noodles, or rice with tomatoes and fresh herbs, or grilled fish or meat served with a starchy vegetable. Each is bathed in a simple sauce or dusted with spices. We've identified the level of difficulty for each recipe (1=easy to 3= complicated) to take the work out of meal planning. While almost all of these dishes are simple to prepare, you'll find some intriguing and challenging recipes, too, like the Avocado Nori Rolls on page 34 and the Stuffed Oriental Pumpkin on page 270.

This book delivers on the promise of its title: Each recipe has five ingredients—with salt and water as extras in just a few. The amount of salt in a recipe is a very personal choice; some people have almost entirely eliminated it from their diets for health reasons, while others give their food a few liberal shakes. So it is a good idea to adjust the salt in these recipes to suit your personal taste. Water is a tricky ingredient to count. You can't cook pasta without water but at the end of the cooking process it gets tossed out; for simplicity's sake, it is not counted as an ingredient at all.

In chapter nine, which features pork, lamb, and beef, be sure to follow your own inclinations for cooking times. For some people, a beef steak that isn't dripping blood is overcooked, while others prefer a blackened surface without a trace of pink inside. However, keep in mind that for health reasons pork absolutely needs to be heated all the way through to at least 160°F (71°C). You may want to invest in a meat thermometer to be sure it is always safely done.

Just 5 Things is divided into 11 easy-to-consult chapters. You'll find dishes for every occasion—from afterschool snacks and light-lunch soups and salads to heartier offerings featuring pasta, noodles, and grains. And if you need crowd-pleasing recipes for family meals or entertaining, there are chapters filled with dishes based on versatile and protein-packed seafood, chicken, meat, and eggs. The finale is a chapter of memorable, mouthwatering desserts.

All 320 recipes have been tested and illustrated by a striking photograph, which will help even novice cooks to prepare and present these simple, gourmet dishes with ease and flair. You'll be surprised by the sheer variety of good food that can be prepared with a minimum of ingredients—and fuss!

# SNACKS

# BLUEBERRY SMOOTHIE

Purée the blueberries in a food processor or blender. • Add the milk, yogurt, honey, and ice. Blend until smooth and thick. • Pour into two large glasses. • Serve.

**3½ cups (500 g) fresh blueberries**
**1 cup (250 ml) milk**
**½ cup (125 ml) thick, Greek-style yogurt**
**2 teaspoons (10 ml) honey**
**10 ice cubes, crushed**

**Serves: 2**
**Preparation: 10 minutes**
**Level: 1**

# CHOCOLATE AND BANANA SMOOTHIE

Cut the bananas into pieces and put in a food processor or blender. • Add the milk, yogurt, chocolate syrup, and ice. Blend until smooth and thick. • Pour the smoothie into two large glasses. • Serve at once.

**2 large ripe bananas**
**1 cup (250 ml) milk**
**½ cup (125 ml) vanilla yogurt**
**¼ cup (60 ml) chocolate syrup or topping**
**10 ice cubes, crushed**

**Serves: 2**
**Preparation: 10 minutes**
**Level: 1**

■ ■ ■ *Use your favorite store-bought chocolate syrup or ice cream topping to make this smoothie. Most come in plastic bottles with nozzles. Squeeze extra syrup around the sides of the empty glasses to add flavor and to make your smoothie look even more enticing.*

# STRAWBERRY SMOOTHIE

Reserve two strawberries for garnish and purée the remaining strawberries in a food processor or blender. • Add the milk, yogurt, cinnamon, and ice. Blend until smooth and thick. • Pour into two large glasses. Slice the reserved strawberries and garnish each glass. • Serve at once.

**3½ cups (500 g) strawberries, hulled**
**1 cup (250 ml) milk**
**½ cup (125 ml) vanilla yogurt**
**½ teaspoon ground cinnamon**
**10 ice cubes, crushed**

**Serves: 2**
**Preparation: 5 minutes**
**Level: 1**

# MANGO SMOOTHIE

Purée the mango in a food processor or blender. • Add the coconut milk, lime juice, yogurt, and ice. Blend until smooth and thick. • Pour into two large glasses. • Serve at once.

**1 pound (500 g) fresh or frozen mango flesh, thawed, if frozen**
**1/3 cup (90 ml) freshly squeezed lime juice**
**1 cup (250 ml) coconut milk**
**1/4 cup (60 g) thick Greek-style yogurt**
**10 ice cubes**

**Serves: 2**
**Preparation: 10 minutes**
**Level: 1**

■ ■ ■ *Fresh mangoes are rich in vitamins A and C. If preferred, replace the mangoes in this smoothie with juicy yellow peaches, peeled, pitted, and chopped into chunks.*

# GOAT CHEESE AND MINT TARTS

Line four small tart pans with the short-crust pastry. Refrigerate for 10 minutes. • Preheat the oven to 300°F (150°C/gas 2). • Remove the pastry from the refrigerator. Cover each pastry shell with a square of waxed paper and fill with 1 tablespoon of uncooked rice. • Place in the oven and bake blind for about 10 minutes, until pastry has just begun to color. • Turn the oven temperature up to 350°F (180°C/gas 4). • Whisk the eggs in a medium bowl. • Add the chopped goat cheese and mint and stir well to combine. • Fill the tart shells with this filling. Season to taste with cracked pepper. • Bake for about 10 minutes, until the filling turns golden. • Serve warm or at room temperature, garnished with the mint leaves.

**2 sheets frozen short-crust pie pastry, thawed**

**3 large eggs**

**8 ounces (250 g) soft goat cheese, crumbled**

**3 tablespoons coarsely chopped fresh mint leaves + whole leaves to garnish**

**Cracked pepper**

**Serves: 4**
**Preparation: 15 minutes + 10 minutes to chill**
**Cooking: 20 minutes**
**Level: 1**

# SHRIMP AND WATERCRESS OPEN SANDWICH

Finely dice the shrimp and combine with the mayonnaise in a small bowl. • Add cracked pepper to taste. • Spread the shrimp mixture on one slice of bread. • Top with the watercress. • Cut in half or quarters. Serve at once.

**3 large shrimp (prawns), cooked, peeled, and deveined**

**2 tablespoons (30 ml) mayonnaise**

**Cracked pepper**

**1 slice white sandwich bread**

**1/4 cup watercress sprigs**

**Serves: 1**
**Preparation: 10 minutes**
**Level: 1**

# STUFFED POTATO WITH BACON AND MUSHROOMS

Preheat the oven to 375°F (190°C/gas 5). • Place the potato on a baking sheet and prick several times with a fork. • Bake for about 1 hour, until tender. • Sauté the bacon in a small frying pan over medium heat for 3 minutes. • Add the mushrooms and cook until they have softened, about 3 minutes. • Remove from the heat and stir in the scallions. • Cut a cross in the top of the baked potato and press the sides together to open. • Fill the potato with the bacon and mushroom mixture. • Top with sour cream. • Serve hot.

- **1 large potato, with peel, scrubbed**
- **1 large slice Canadian bacon (lean bacon), cut into small pieces**
- **4 button mushrooms, thinly sliced**
- **1 tablespoon sliced scallions (green onions, spring onions)**
- **2 tablespoons sour cream**

**Serves: 1**
**Preparation: 10 minutes**
**Cooking: 1 hour 10 minutes**
**Level: 1**

# CHEESE AND SWEET POTATO PASTIES

Preheat the oven to 425°F (220°C/gas 7). Line a large baking sheet with parchment paper. • Dice the sweet potatoes into 1/2-inch (1-cm) cubes. • Place in a steamer over a saucepan of boiling water. Steam until soft, about 5 minutes. • Combine the sweet potatoes, ricotta, Parmesan, and pesto in a medium bowl. • Lay the pastry sheets on a clean work surface and cut out four large circles. • Divide the sweet potato mixture into four equal portions. Place in the center of each pastry circle. • Fold the pastry over the filling to make a half-moon shape. Pinch the edges together and seal with a little water. • Place the pasties on the prepared baking sheet and lightly brush the tops with water. • Bake for about 25 minutes, until pale golden brown. • Serve hot.

- **2 medium sweet potatoes, peeled**
- **3/4 cup (180 g) ricotta cheese, drained**
- **1/4 cup (30 g) freshly grated Parmesan cheese**
- **2 tablespoons basil pesto**
- **2 sheets frozen puff pastry, thawed**

**Serves: 4**
**Preparation: 20 minutes**
**Cooking: 30 minutes**
**Level: 1**

# AVOCADO NORI ROLLS

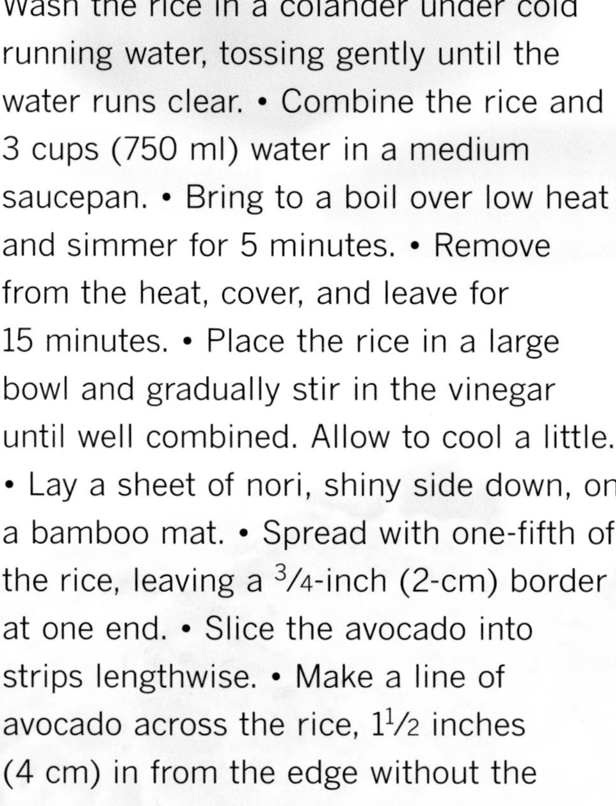

Wash the rice in a colander under cold running water, tossing gently until the water runs clear. • Combine the rice and 3 cups (750 ml) water in a medium saucepan. • Bring to a boil over low heat and simmer for 5 minutes. • Remove from the heat, cover, and leave for 15 minutes. • Place the rice in a large bowl and gradually stir in the vinegar until well combined. Allow to cool a little. • Lay a sheet of nori, shiny side down, on a bamboo mat. • Spread with one-fifth of the rice, leaving a 3/4-inch (2-cm) border at one end. • Slice the avocado into strips lengthwise. • Make a line of avocado across the rice, 1½ inches (4 cm) in from the edge without the

**2½ cups (500 g) short-grain white rice**
**5 nori sheets**
**¼ cup (60 ml) rice wine vinegar**
**1 avocado, halved and pitted (stoned)**
**½ cup (125 ml) soy sauce**

**Serves: 4**
**Preparation: 35 minutes**
**Cooking: 20 minutes**
**Level: 2**

■ ■ ■ Nori *is the Japanese word for several species of edible seaweed and also for the food products derived from them. Nori sheets are a common wrap for sushi. They are widely available in natural food stores as well as in the Asian section of your supermarket or local specialty food store.*

border. • Roll the mat over to enclose the avocado and continue rolling to form a firm roll. Use a little water to seal the seam. • Repeat this same process with the remaining nori sheets. • Trim the ends and cut each roll into six slices. Serve with the soy sauce for dipping.

# EGGPLANT DIP WITH TOASTED PITA

Preheat the oven to 400°F (200°C/ gas 6). • Place the eggplant on a baking sheet and pierce in few places with a fork. • Bake for about 1 hour, until softened. • Allow the eggplant to cool a little. Remove and discard the skin and coarsely chop the flesh. • Place the flesh in a sieve and squeeze out any excess liquid. • Using a fork, mash eggplant in a medium-sized bowl. • Add the oil, lemon juice, and garlic. Stir well to combine. • Place in a serving bowl. • Serve with toasted pita bread.

**1 medium (about 1 pound/500 g) eggplant (aubergine)**

**3 tablespoons (45 ml) extra-virgin olive oil**

**2 tablespoons (30 ml) freshly squeezed lemon juice**

**2 cloves garlic, finely chopped**

**4 pita breads, sliced into wedges and toasted**

**Serves: 2–4**
**Preparation: 10 minutes**
**Cooking: 1 hour**
**Level: 1**

# PORK DUMPLINGS

Combine the pork, hoisin, and scallions in a medium bowl. • Place a heaped tablespoon of pork mixture in the center of each wonton wrapper. • Brush a little water around the edges of the wrappers and fold over the mixture, pressing to seal. If using round wonton wrappers fold into semicircles; if using square wrappers, fold into triangles. • Line a large steamer with waxed paper. Make holes in it so that the steam can come through. • Place the dumplings on top in a single layer and cover with a lid. • Place the steamer over a saucepan of boiling water. • Steam until the dumplings are cooked through, 8–10 minutes. • Serve hot with soy sauce for dipping.

- **1 pound (500 g) ground (minced) pork**
- **1/4 cup (60 ml) hoisin sauce**
- **3 tablespoons finely chopped scallions (green onions, spring onions)**
- **20 round wonton wrappers**
- **1/2 cup (125 ml) soy sauce**

**Serves: 4**
**Preparation: 35 minutes**
**Cooking: 10 minutes**
**Level: 2**

■■■ *Wonton wrappers are thin round or square sheets of dough used to make Asian dumplings and other appetizers. They are widely available in well-stocked supermarkets and Asian food stores. In this recipe, substitute square wonton wrappers if round ones are unavailable.*

# STEAMED SHRIMP DUMPLINGS

Put the shrimp in a food processor and process until coarsely chopped. • In a medium bowl, combine the shrimp, ginger, cilantro, and 1 tablespoon of the soy sauce. • Place a heaping tablespoon of the shrimp mixture in the center of a wonton wrapper. Bring the sides up around the outside and form pleats to firmly encase the filling. The top of the dumpling should be exposed. • Repeat with the remaining wrappers. • Line a large steamer with waxed paper. Make holes in it so that the steam can come through. • Place the dumplings on top in a single layer and cover with a lid. • Place the steamer over a saucepan of boiling water. • Steam until the dumplings are cooked through, 8–10 minutes. • Serve hot with the remaining soy sauce for dipping.

- **1 pound (500 g) shrimp (prawns), shelled and deveined**
- **3 tablespoons pickled ginger, finely sliced**
- **3 tablespoons coarsely chopped fresh cilantro (coriander)**
- **½ cup (125 ml) soy sauce**
- **20 wonton wrappers**

**Serves: 4**
**Preparation: 40 minutes**
**Cooking: 10 minutes**
**Level: 2**

■ ■ ■ *Pickled ginger, usually preserved in rice wine, is deliciously sweet and slightly spicy. You can buy it in Asian food stores.*

# CARAMELIZED ONION AND SPINACH TARTS

Combine the onions and oil in a heavy saucepan over low heat and simmer, stirring often, until caramelized, about 30 minutes. • Line four small fluted tart pans with short-crust pastry. Refrigerate for 10 minutes. • Preheat the oven to 300°F (150°C/gas 2). • Remove the pastry from the refrigerator. Cover each pastry shell with a square of waxed paper and fill with 1 tablespoon of rice. Place in the oven and blind bake for about 10 minutes, until the pastry has just begun to color. • Turn the oven temperature up to 350°F (180°C/gas 4). • Combine the onions, spinach, and salt in a medium bowl. • Fill the tart shells with spinach and onion filling. • Bake for 10 more minutes, or until the pastry is pale golden brown. • Serve hot or at room temperature.

**4 large yellow onions, sliced**

**2 tablespoons extra-virgin olive oil**

**2 sheets frozen short-crust pie pastry, thawed**

**4 large handfuls baby spinach leaves**

**1/2 teaspoon salt**

**Serves: 4**
**Preparation: 15 minutes + 10 minutes to chill**
**Cooking: 50 minutes**
**Level: 1**

# AVOCADO AND BACON BURRITO

Fry the bacon in a large frying pan over medium-high heat until crisp, about 6 minutes. • Slice the avocado halves lengthwise into 4–6 pieces. • Heat the tortillas in a frying pan one at a time until they begin to color. • Lay the tortillas on a clean work surface and spread with the salsa. • Evenly divide the avocado, bacon, and spinach among the tortillas. • Fold to enclose the filling. • Serve hot.

- **8 slices bacon, rind removed, if necessary**
- **2 avocados, halved and pitted (stoned)**
- **1½ cups baby spinach leaves**
- **4 flour tortillas**
- **⅓ cup (90 ml) salsa or fruit chutney**

**Serves: 4**
**Preparation: 5 minutes**
**Cooking: 10 minutes**
**Level: 1**

# GUACAMOLE WITH CORN CHIPS

Dice the avocado. Place in a medium bowl and use a fork to roughly mash. • Add the onion, olives, and lemon juice. Stir well to combine. • Transfer the guacamole to a small serving bowl. Serve with the corn chips.

- **2 avocados, halved and pitted (stoned)**
- **1 small red onion, finely diced**
- **¼ cup (50 g) pitted black olives, diced**
- **3 tablespoons (45 ml) freshly squeezed lemon juice**
- **Corn chips, to serve**

**Serves: 2**
**Preparation: 10 minutes**
**Level: 1**

# SAUSAGE ROLLS

Preheat the oven to 425°F (220°C/gas 7). Line a large baking sheet with parchment paper. • Combine the sausage meat, onion, thyme, and 1/3 cup (90 g) of the chutney in a medium bowl. • Lay the pastry sheets out on a clean work surface and cut in half lengthwise. • Place the sausage mixture in a piping bag with a large plain tip. • Pipe a line of mixture down the center of each pastry sheet. Add additional mixture if necessary until all is used. • Roll the pastry around the sausage meat and seal the edges. Brush the tops with a little water. • Cut each log in half and prick the tops with a fork. • Place the sausage rolls seam-side down on the prepared baking sheet. • Bake for 15–20 minutes, until golden brown. • Serve hot with the remaining chutney.

- **2 sheets puff pastry**
- **1 pound (500 g) sausage meat**
- **1 onion, finely diced**
- **2 tablespoons finely chopped fresh thyme**
- **1 cup (250 g) fruit chutney**

**Serves: 4**
**Preparation: 15 minutes**
**Cooking: 15–20 minutes**
**Level: 1**

# CHICKEN RICE PAPER ROLLS

Place the noodles in a medium bowl and soak in hot water until soft, about 5 minutes. • Drain, roughly chop into shorter lengths, and return to the bowl. • Add the chicken, mint, and 1 tablespoon of chili sauce and combine well. • Soak the rice paper wrappers one at a time in a large bowl of warm water until they soften, about 2 minutes. • Lay the softened sheets on a clean work surface. • Place about 1 tablespoon of the filling mixture along the bottom third of the wrapper, allowing enough space at the sides to fold over. • Fold the sides inward and firmly roll up the wrapper. • Repeat this process with the remaining wrappers. • Place the rolls, seam side down, on a serving plate. • Serve with remaining chili sauce for dipping.

■■■ *If not serving immediately, cover the rice paper rolls with a clean damp kitchen towel to prevent them from drying out.*

**3 ounces (90 g) vermicelli rice noodles**

**16 rice paper wrappers**

**1 chicken breast, grilled and shredded**

**3 tablespoons finely chopped fresh Vietnamese (or other) mint**

**½ cup (125 ml) Thai sweet chili sauce**

Serves: 4
Preparation: 40 minutes
Level: 1

# CORN FRITTERS

Whisk the egg and corn liquid together in a medium bowl. • Add the corn and flour and stir with a fork until just combined. • Heat the oil in a large frying pan over medium-high heat. • Drop tablespoons of batter into the oil and cook until golden brown, about 3 minutes on each side. • Place the fritters on paper towels to drain off any excess oil. • Serve hot with the chutney for dipping.

- **1 large egg**
- **1 (14-ounce/400-g) can corn (sweet corn) kernels, drained + 1/4 cup (60 ml) of the liquid reserved**
- **1 cup (150 g) self-rising flour**
- **1/4 cup (60 ml) extra-virgin olive oil**
- **1/2 cup (125 g) fruit chutney**

**Serves: 4**
**Preparation: 15 minutes**
**Cooking: 15 minutes**
**Level: 1**

# TOMATO AND FETA CHEESE BRUSCHETTA

Place the tomatoes on a small baking sheet and drizzle with 1 tablespoon of the reserved feta oil. • Place under a hot broiler (grill) and cook until the tomatoes begin to collapse, 3–4 minutes. • Lightly brush the sourdough bread with the remaining oil and broil (grill) until golden. • Combine the tomatoes, feta, and tarragon in a medium bowl. Add cracked pepper to taste. • Arrange the mixture on top of the toasted bread. • Broil for 2 more minutes. Serve hot.

**12 red cherry tomatoes**
**½ cup (120 g) marinated feta, crumbled, with 3 tablespoons (45 ml) of the oil reserved**
**2 thick slices sourdough bread**
**½ tablespoon roughly chopped fresh tarragon**
**Cracked pepper**

**Serves: 1–2**
**Preparation: 5 minutes**
**Cooking: 10 minutes**
**Level: 1**

■ ■ ■ *If preferred, use extra-virgin olive oil and plain feta instead of marinated feta.*

# SALMON CAKES WITH CILANTRO

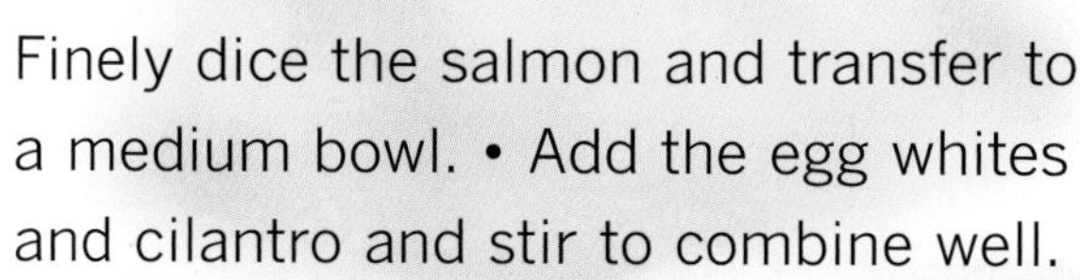

Finely dice the salmon and transfer to a medium bowl. • Add the egg whites and cilantro and stir to combine well. • Heat the oil in a large frying pan over medium-high heat. • Place 2 tablespoons of the salmon mixture in the oil and fry until light golden, about 1 minute on each side. • Repeat with the remaining salmon mixture. • Place the salmon cakes on paper towels to drain off any excess oil. • Serve hot with chili sauce for dipping.

- **1 pound (500 g) salmon fillet, skin and bones removed**
- **2 egg whites, lightly beaten**
- **3 tablespoons finely chopped fresh cilantro (coriander)**
- **1 cup (250 ml) canola oil**
- **½ cup (125 ml) Thai sweet chili sauce**

**Serves: 4**
**Preparation: 10 minutes**
**Cooking: 5 minutes**
**Level: 1**

# EGG AND BACON MUFFIN

Cook the bacon in a medium frying pan over medium heat until crisp, about 5 minutes. Remove and set aside. • Fry the egg in the bacon fat for 3–4 minutes; if liked, turn over and fry the other side for 1 minute. • Toast the muffin or bun and spread with mayonnaise. • Place the lettuce, bacon, and egg on top and cover with the lid. • Serve at once.

- **2 slices Canadian bacon (lean bacon), rind removed, if necessary**
- **1 large egg**
- **1 English muffin or hamburger bun**
- **1 tablespoon (15 ml) mayonnaise**
- **1 lettuce leaf**

**Serves: 1**
**Preparation: 5 minutes**
**Cooking: 10 minutes**
**Level: 1**

# ARTICHOKE AND ARUGULA PIZZAS

Preheat the oven to 400°F (200°C/gas 6). Set out a large baking sheet. • Spread the tomato paste evenly over each pizza crust. • Arrange four artichoke halves on each pizza. • Divide the haloumi evenly and place on top. • Place the pizzas on the baking sheet. Bake for about 15 minutes, until the crust is crisp and golden brown. • Garnish with the arugula and serve hot.

- **4 ready-made 8-inch (20-cm) pizza crusts**
- **1/2 cup (125 ml) tomato paste**
- **8 marinated artichoke hearts, halved**
- **6 ounces (180 g) haloumi cheese, sliced thinly**
- **1/4 cup arugula (rocket) leaves**

**Serves: 4**
**Preparation: 10 minutes**
**Cooking: 15 minutes**
**Level: 1**

■ ■ ■ *Haloumi is a semisoft to firm cooking cheese from Greece, Turkey, and Cyprus. It is preserved in whey and has a slightly salty flavor. Replace with feta cheese, if preferred.*

# PANCETTA, ARUGULA, AND TOMATO SANDWICH

Fry the pancetta in a medium frying pan until crisp, about 5–6 minutes. • Slice the bread in half horizontally. Toast the outsides under a broiler (grill) until golden, about 3 minutes each. • To assemble: spread the bread base with the mayonnaise. Lay the arugula, pancetta, and tomato on top and cover with the lid. • Serve hot.

- **3** **slices pancetta (or bacon)**
- **1** **small Turkish bread roll or ciabatta**
- **2** **tablespoons (30 ml) mayonnaise**
- **1** **tomato, sliced**
- **½** **cup arugula (rocket) leaves**

**Serves: 1**
**Preparation: 5 minutes**
**Cooking: 10 minutes**
**Level: 1**

# HUMMUS WITH TOASTED TURKISH BREAD

Place the chickpeas and reserved liquid, garlic, lemon juice, and tahini in a food processor. • Blend until smooth and well combined. • Place the hummus in a small serving bowl. • Serve with the toasted bread.

**1** **(14-ounce/400-g) can chickpeas, drained with 3 tablespoons (45 ml) of the liquid reserved**

**2** **cloves garlic, chopped**

**3** **tablespoons (45 ml) freshly squeezed lemon juice**

**¼** **cup (60 ml) tahini**

**12** **slices Turkish bread or focaccia, toasted**

**Serves: 2–4**
**Preparation: 10 minutes**
**Level: 1**

■ ■ ■ *This classic Middle Eastern dish makes a healthy snack or appetizer. Tahini is a thick paste made from crushed sesame seeds. Buy it at an ethnic food store or in the Middle Eastern foods section of your local supermarket.*

# OLIVE AND OREGANO PIZZA

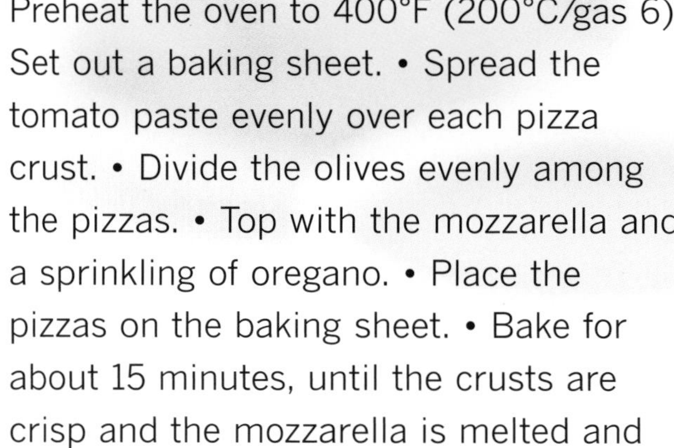

Preheat the oven to 400°F (200°C/gas 6). Set out a baking sheet. • Spread the tomato paste evenly over each pizza crust. • Divide the olives evenly among the pizzas. • Top with the mozzarella and a sprinkling of oregano. • Place the pizzas on the baking sheet. • Bake for about 15 minutes, until the crusts are crisp and the mozzarella is melted and spread. • Serve hot.

- **½ cup (125 ml) tomato paste**
- **4 ready-made 8-inch (20-cm) pizza crusts**
- **¾ cup (150 g) pitted black olives**
- **4 small mozzarella cheeses (about 5 ounces/150 g), thinly sliced**
- **4 tablespoons dried oregano**

Serves: 4
Preparation: 10 minutes
Cooking: 15 minutes
Level: 1

# BEET DIP WITH BAGEL CHIPS

Cook the beets in a large saucepan of boiling water until tender, about 45 minutes. • Drain and allow to cool a little. • Wearing food-handling gloves, peel the beets. • Coarsely chop the beets and place in a food processor. • Add the yogurt, lemon juice, and cumin. Blend until smooth and well combined. • Place the beet dip in a small serving bowl. Serve with bagel chips.

**3** **medium (about 1 pound/500 g) beets (beetroot/red beet), trimmed**

**3/4** **cup (200 g) plain yogurt**

**2** **tablespoons (30 ml) freshly squeezed lemon juice**

**1** **teaspoon ground cumin**

**Bagel chips, to serve**

Serves: 2–4
Preparation: 10 minutes
Cooking: 45 minutes
Level: 1

■ ■ ■ *Dark red beets will stain your hands if you peel them without gloves. If you stain your hands, you can remove the stains by slicing a potato in half and rubbing it over the stains under cold running water.*

# POLENTA CHIPS WITH TOMATO SALSA

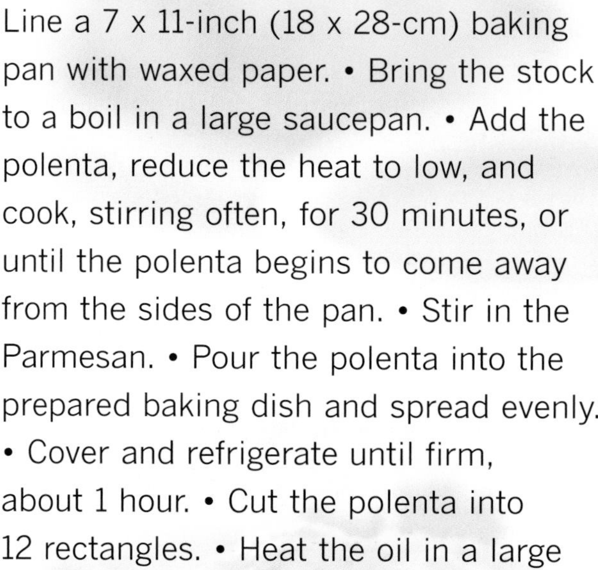

Line a 7 x 11-inch (18 x 28-cm) baking pan with waxed paper. • Bring the stock to a boil in a large saucepan. • Add the polenta, reduce the heat to low, and cook, stirring often, for 30 minutes, or until the polenta begins to come away from the sides of the pan. • Stir in the Parmesan. • Pour the polenta into the prepared baking dish and spread evenly. • Cover and refrigerate until firm, about 1 hour. • Cut the polenta into 12 rectangles. • Heat the oil in a large frying pan. • Fry the polenta until light brown and crisp on all sides. • Place on paper towels to drain off any excess oil. • Serve hot with the tomato salsa.

**8 cups (2 liters) vegetable stock**

**2 cups (400 g) polenta**

**3/4 cup (120 g) freshly grated Parmesan cheese**

**1 cup (250 ml) extra-virgin olive oil**

**1 cup (250 ml) tomato salsa**

Serves: 4
Preparation: 15 minutes + 1 hour to firm the polenta
Cooking: 40 minutes
Level: 2

# DUCK AND SNOW PEA WRAPS

Place the duck in a small frying pan over medium heat, skin side down. Cook until browned and cooked through, 8–10 minutes on each side. • Remove the fat and thinly slice the meat. • Heat the tortillas one at a time in a frying pan over medium until they begin to color. • Lay the hot tortillas on a clean work surface and spread with the hoisin sauce. • Evenly divide the duck, snow peas, and cucumber among the tortillas. • Fold to enclose the filling. Serve hot.

- **1 boneless duck breast**
- **2 small flour tortillas**
- **1/4 cup (60 ml) hoisin sauce**
- **10 snow peas (sugar peas/mangetout), trimmed and finely sliced lengthwise**
- **1 small cucumber, finely sliced lengthwise**

**Serves: 2**
**Preparation: 10 minutes**
**Cooking: 20 minutes**
**Level: 1**

■ ■ ■ *Hoisin sauce, also known as Peking sauce, is a thick, sweet, and spicy mixture of soybeans, salt, garlic, chilies, and other spices. Buy it at an ethnic food store or in the Asian foods section of your local supermarket.*

# CAJUN POTATO WEDGES

Preheat oven to 375°F (190°C/gas 5). • Pour the oil into a large baking dish. Place in the oven for 5 minutes, or until hot. • Cut the potatoes into wedges and roll in the Cajun spice mix. • Add the potatoes to the hot oil and toss to coat well. • Bake for 25–30 minutes, until golden, turning occasionally. • Serve hot with the sour cream and salsa for dipping.

- **½ cup (125 ml) vegetable oil**
- **4 medium potatoes, peeled**
- **2 tablespoons Cajun spice mix**
- **½ cup (125 ml) sour cream**
- **½ cup (125 g) tomato salsa**

**Serves: 4**
**Preparation: 10 minutes**
**Cooking: 25–30 minutes**
**Level: 1**

■ ■ ■ *Cajun spice mix is usually made with a mixture of salt, pepper, chile powder, paprika, ground cumin, and thyme. Substitute any highly flavored spice or barbecue mix you have on hand.*

# SMOKED SALMON FILO PARCELS

Preheat the oven to 425°F (220°C/gas 7). Lightly butter a baking sheet. • Rinse the spinach under cold running water. Do not drain but place in a saucepan over medium-high heat with the water clinging to the leaves. Stir often and cook until the leaves are wilted and bright green, 3–5 minutes. • Let cool a little, then gently squeeze out the excess moisture. Chop coarsely with a large knife. • Combine the salmon, spinach, and crème fraîche in a medium bowl. • Place one sheet of pastry on a clean work surface. • Using a pastry brush, paint the sheet with melted butter and lay another sheet on top. Cut in half lengthwise. • Place a quarter of the salmon mixture at the top of a pastry sheet. • Fold the pastry over to form a triangular shape and continue folding down to the end. Seal and brush the top with a little melted butter. • Repeat this process with the remaining filling mixture and pastry. • Place the

**2 cups baby spinach leaves**

**4 slices smoked salmon, chopped**

**½ cup (125 ml) crème fraîche or sour cream**

**4 sheets phyllo (filo) pastry**

**¼ cup (60 g) butter, melted**

Serves: 2
Preparation: 25 minutes
Cooking: 30 minutes
Level: 1

parcels on the prepared baking sheet. Bake for 20–25 minutes, until the pastry is golden and crisp. • Serve hot or at room temperature.



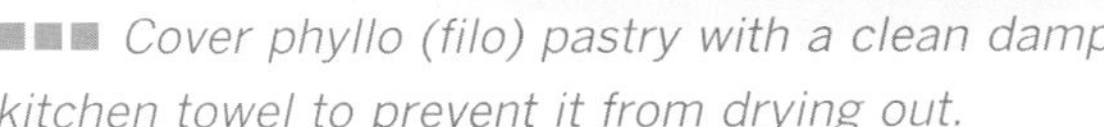

*Cover phyllo (filo) pastry with a clean damp kitchen towel to prevent it from drying out.*

# SOUPS

# TOMATO AND TARRAGON SOUP

Preheat the oven to 350°F (180°C/gas 4). • Place the tomatoes on a baking sheet. Bake for about 20 minutes, until the tomatoes are soft and begin to collapse. Remove the skins and set aside. • Peel the onions and place on a separate baking sheet. Bake for about 25 minutes, until light golden in color. • Combine the tomatoes, onions, stock, and sugar in a medium saucepan. Bring to a boil and then reduce to a simmer. • Add the tarragon and simmer for 5 minutes. • Purée the soup with a hand-held blender or in a food processor. • Return to the heat for 2–3 minutes. Serve hot.

**12 large tomatoes**
**4 medium yellow onions**
**3 cups (750 ml) vegetable stock**
**1½ teaspoons sugar**
**3 tablespoons finely chopped fresh tarragon**

**Serves: 4**
**Preparation: 10 minutes**
**Cooking: About 1 hour**
**Level: 1**

■ ■ ■ *The baked onions give this soup a deliciously sweet flavor. If preferred, replace the tarragon with the same quantity of finely chopped basil.*

# MINTY PEA SOUP

Chop the peas in a food processor until smooth. Put in a medium saucepan. • Add the stock, mint, and crumbled goat cheese. • Bring to a boil over medium heat and simmer gently for 5 minutes. • Ladle into bowls and garnish with the extra goat cheese and mint leaves. Serve hot.

- **$2\frac{1}{2}$ cups (400 g) frozen peas, thawed**
- **4 cups (1 liter) vegetable stock**
- **3 tablespoons finely sliced mint + extra leaves to garnish**
- **3 ounces (90 g) goat cheese + extra to garnish**

Serves: 4
Preparation: 10 minutes
Cooking: 10 minutes
Level: 1

# GINGER CHICKEN SOUP

Combine the stock, chicken breasts, and ginger in a large saucepan. • Bring to a boil and simmer gently for 15 minutes. • Reduce the heat and remove the chicken breasts. • Add the carrot and soy sauce to the pan. • Shred the chicken and divide evenly among four serving bowls. Pour the soup over the top and serve hot.

**5 cups (1.25 liters) chicken stock**

**2 small boneless, skinless chicken breasts**

**1½ tablespoons grated fresh ginger**

**2 large carrots, grated**

**2 tablespoons (30 ml) soy sauce**

Serves: 4
Preparation: 10 minutes
Cooking: 20 minutes
Level: 1

# SPICY SAUSAGE AND TOMATO SOUP

Combine the stock, tomatoes, sausage, and beans in a large saucepan. • Bring to a boil and simmer gently for 10 minutes. • Add the thyme and simmer for 5 more minutes. • Serve hot.



- **2 cups (500 ml) vegetable stock**
- **2 (14-ounce/400-g) cans chopped tomatoes, with juice**
- **8 ounces (250 g) Spanish chorizo sausage, peeled and sliced**
- **1 (14-ounce/400-g) can cannellini beans, drained**
- **2 tablespoons coarsely chopped fresh thyme**

**Serves: 4**
**Preparation: 10 minutes**
**Cooking: 15 minutes**
**Level: 1**

■ ■ ■ *Chorizo is a spicy sausage made in Mexico or Spain. Spanish chorizo is made with smoked pork while Mexican chorizo is made with fresh pork. If preferred, replace the Spanish chorizo with another type of highly seasoned sausage.*

# ROASTED BELL PEPPER SOUP

Preheat the oven to 400°F (200°C/gas 6). • Place the bell peppers on a baking sheet. • Roast until the skins begin to blister and blacken, about 30 minutes. • Remove the bell peppers from the oven and place in a small bowl. • Cover with plastic wrap (cling film) and allow to cool for 10 minutes. • Remove the seeds and skins from the bell peppers. • Slice into quarters. • Combine the bell peppers, chicken stock, onions, tomatoes, and garlic in a large saucepan. • Bring to a boil and simmer for 15 minutes.
• Purée the soup with a hand-held blender or in a food processor.
• Reheat the soup for 2–3 minutes, then serve hot.

**5 medium red bell peppers (capsicums)**
**4 cups (1 liter) chicken stock**
**2 yellow onions, quartered**
**1 (14-ounce/400-g) can chopped tomatoes, with juice**
**2 cloves garlic, chopped**

Serves: 4
Preparation: 30 minutes + 10 minutes to cool
Cooking: 50 minutes
Level: 2

# SWEET POTATO SOUP

Combine the sweet potatoes and vegetable stock in a large saucepan over medium heat. Bring to a boil. • Simmer for 15 minutes, or until the potatoes are soft. • Purée with a hand-held blender or in a food processor. • Return to the heat and add the coconut milk, lime juice, and chilies. • Gently simmer for 5 more minutes. • Serve hot.

- **2 pounds (1 kg) sweet potatoes, peeled and coarsely chopped**
- **3 cups (750 ml) vegetable stock**
- **1 (14-ounce/400-ml) can coconut milk**
- **1/4 cup (60 ml) freshly squeezed lime juice**
- **2 small fresh red chilies, seeded and finely sliced**

Serves: 4
Preparation: 15 minutes
Cooking: 20 minutes
Level: 1

# CORN SOUP

Heat the butter in a large saucepan over medium heat. • Add the corn and onion and simmer for 5 minutes. • Add the chicken stock and bring to a boil. Simmer for 10 minutes, or until the corn is tender. • Add the cream and simmer gently for 5 more minutes. • Purée with a hand-held blender or in a food processor. • Reheat the soup for 2–3 minutes, then serve hot.

- **1/4 cup (60 g) butter**
- **Kernels from 5 ears (cobs) corn (sweet corn)**
- **2 large onions, sliced**
- **4 cups (1 liter) chicken stock**
- **1/2 cup (125 ml) light (single) cream**

**Serves: 4**
**Preparation: 10 minutes**
**Cooking: 20 minutes**
**Level: 1**

# CREAM OF FENNEL SOUP

Combine the leeks, fennel, and chicken stock in a large saucepan over medium heat. Bring to a boil and simmer for 15 minutes, or until the fennel and leeks are tender. • Add the cream and simmer gently for 5 more minutes. • Purée with a hand-held blender or in a food processor. • Reheat the soup for 2–3 minutes. Stir in the lemon juice and ladle into preheated serving bowls. Garnish with the lemon zest and serve hot.

**2 leeks, white part only, coarsely chopped**

**1 bulb (about 1 pound/500 g) fennel, thinly sliced**

**3 cups (750 ml) chicken stock**

**2 cups (500 ml) light (single) cream**

**3 tablespoons (45 ml) freshly squeezed lemon juice + finely sliced lemon zest, to garnish**

**Serves: 4**
**Preparation: 15 minutes**
**Cooking: 25 minutes**
**Level: 1**

■ ■ ■ *Fennel and leeks are both winter vegetables. Serve this creamy soup piping hot on cold winter days.*

# POTATO SOUP

Heat the butter in a large saucepan over medium heat. Add the onions and sauté until they are transparent, about 5 minutes. • Add the potatoes and garlic and sauté for 5 more minutes. • Add the chicken stock and bring to a boil. Simmer for 15 minutes, or until the potatoes are tender. • Purée with a hand-held blender or in a food processor. • Reheat the soup for 2–3 minutes, then serve hot.

- **1/3 cup (90 g) butter**
- **4 medium onions, sliced**
- **2 pounds (1 kg) potatoes, peeled and cubed**
- **4 cloves garlic, finely chopped**
- **3 cups (750 ml) chicken stock**

Serves: 4
Preparation: 15 minutes
Cooking: 30 minutes
Level: 1

# CABBAGE AND POTATO SOUP

Heat the oil in a large saucepan over medium-low heat. Add the cabbage and sauté for 10 minutes. • Slice the potatoes thinly into wedges and add to the cabbage. • Add the chicken stock and bring to a boil. • Simmer until potatoes are tender, about 10 minutes. • Add the parsley and serve hot.

- **1/4 cup (60 ml) walnut oil**
- **1/4 Savoy cabbage (about 2 pounds/ 1 kg), cored and thinly shredded**
- **1 pound (500 g) potatoes, scrubbed, with peel**
- **5 cups (1.25 liters) chicken stock**
- **1/3 cup coarsely chopped fresh parsley**

**Serves: 4**
**Preparation: 10 minutes**
**Cooking: 25 minutes**
**Level: 1**

■ ■ ■ *Walnut oil will add a delicious nutty flavor to this soup. You may replace it with the same amount of extra-virgin olive oil, if preferred.*

# ASPARAGUS AND CRÈME FRAÎCHE SOUP

Add the asparagus spears to a pot of boiling water and cook for 2 minutes. • Refresh in cold water to stop the cooking process and set aside. • Combine the stock, potatoes, and leeks in a large saucepan and bring to a boil. Simmer gently for 10 minutes. • Set eight asparagus spears aside to garnish and add the rest to the saucepan. Simmer for 5 minutes, or until the asparagus and potatoes are tender. • Purée using a hand-held blender or in a food processor. • Strain the mixture through a fine sieve. • Return to the heat and stir in the crème fraîche. Garnish with the reserved asparagus spears and serve hot.

- **1¼ pounds (600 g) asparagus, woody ends removed**
- **3 cups (750 ml) chicken stock**
- **1 pound (500 g) potatoes, peeled and cubed**
- **2 leeks, white part only, thinly sliced**
- **⅔ cup (150 g) crème fraîche or sour cream**

**Serves: 4**
**Preparation: 25 minutes**
**Cooking: 20 minutes**
**Level: 1**

# SQUASH AND PANCETTA SOUP

Place the pancetta in a large saucepan over medium heat and fry until crisp. • Remove the pancetta and drain on paper towels. • Add the onion and garlic to the remaining oil in the saucepan and sauté for 3 minutes, or until just tender. • Add the squash and stock and bring to the boil. • Simmer for 12 minutes, or until the squash is tender. • Purée with a hand-held blender or in a food processor. • Return to the heat, add the pancetta, and reheat for 2–3 minutes. Serve hot.

- **8 ounces (250 g) sliced pancetta, coarsely chopped**
- **1 onion, finely chopped**
- **3 cloves garlic, coarsely chopped**
- **2 pounds (1 kg) butternut squash (pumpkin), peeled, seeded, and coarsely chopped**
- **5 cups (1.25 liters) chicken stock**

**Serves: 4**
**Preparation: 15 minutes**
**Cooking: 25 minutes**
**Level: 1**

# TOMATO AND LIMA BEAN SOUP

Combine the vegetable stock and zucchini in a large saucepan over medium heat and bring to a boil. Simmer for 5 minutes. • Add the tomato soup, butter beans, and oregano and bring back to a boil. • Simmer gently for 10 minutes. • Serve hot.

- **2 cups (500 ml) vegetable stock**
- **2 zucchini, diced**
- **2 (10¾-ounce/300-g) cans condensed tomato soup**
- **2 (10-ounce/300-g) cans lima beans or butter beans, drained**
- **2 tablespoons finely chopped fresh oregano**

**Serves: 4**
**Preparation: 10 minutes**
**Cooking: 15 minutes**
**Level: 1**

# CHICKEN NOODLE SOUP

Combine the stock, chicken breasts, and mushrooms in a large saucepan over medium heat. Bring to a boil and simmer gently for 15 minutes. • Reduce the heat and remove the chicken breasts. • Add the noodles and scallions and simmer for 5 minutes. • Shred the chicken and return to the soup. • Serve hot.

**5 cups (1.25 liters) chicken stock**

**2 small boneless, skinless chicken breasts**

**4 ounces (125 g) shiitake mushroom caps, sliced**

**5 ounces (150 g) vermicelli pasta**

**2 scallions (green onions, spring onions), green tips only, thinly sliced**

Serves: 4
Preparation: 15 minutes
Cooking: 25 minutes
Level: 1

# CARROT AND CILANTRO SOUP

Use a sharp knife to remove the zest from the oranges—outer orange part only. Slice thinly. Juice the oranges. • Combine the carrots, onion, orange juice, and zest in a large saucepan over medium heat. • Add 2 cups (500 ml) of the stock and bring to a boil. Simmer for 10 minutes. • Add the chopped cilantro to the soup. • Purée using a hand-held blender or in a food processor. • Add the remaining 2 cups (500 ml) of stock to the soup and return to the heat. Simmer gently for 5 minutes. • Garnish with the extra cilantro leaves and serve hot.

**2 oranges**
**1 pound (500 g) carrots, grated**
**1 large onion, sliced**
**4 cups (1 liter) vegetable stock**
**1/2 cup finely chopped fresh cilantro (coriander) + extra leaves to garnish**

**Serves: 4**
**Preparation: 15 minutes**
**Cooking: 20–25 minutes**
**Level: 1**

# YOGURT AND CUCUMBER SOUP

Scoop out the seeds of the cucumbers with a teaspoon and discard. • Grate the cucumbers and place in a large bowl. • Add the yogurt and purée with a hand-held blender or in a food processor. • Stir in the mint and dill and season to taste with salt. • Refrigerate the soup for at least 30 minutes to allow the flavors to infuse. • Serve cold.

- **4 cucumbers, peeled and halved lengthwise**
- **3 cups (750 g) plain yogurt**
- **2 tablespoons finely chopped fresh mint**
- **2 tablespoons finely chopped fresh dill**
- **Salt**

Serves: 4
Preparation: 15 minutes + 30 minutes to infuse
Level: 1

■ ■ ■ *This refreshing soup is perfect for hot summer days. Keep the cucumbers and yogurt in the refrigerator until just before you prepare the soup and serve cool.*

# RED LENTIL SOUP

Combine the lentils, potatoes, and onions in a large saucepan over medium heat. Add the stock and bring to a boil. • Simmer gently for 20–25 minutes, until the lentils and potatoes are tender. • Purée using a hand-held blender or in a food processor. • Season with pepper and reheat the soup for 2–3 minutes. Serve hot.

- **1 cup (100 g) red lentils, rinsed**
- **8 medium potatoes, peeled and cubed**
- **2 onions, finely sliced**
- **5 cups (1.25 liters) chicken stock**
- **Freshly ground white pepper**

**Serves: 4**
**Preparation: 15 minutes**
**Cooking: 30 minutes**
**Level: 1**

# WATERCRESS SOUP

Combine the watercress, onions, and stock in a large saucepan over medium heat. Bring to a boil. • Simmer gently for 10 minutes, or until the watercress is tender. • Purée with a hand-held blender or in a food processor. • Return to the heat and stir in the sour cream. • Season with cracked pepper to taste. Garnish with the extra sprigs of watercress and serve hot.

- **1 pound (500 g) watercress, + extra sprigs to garnish**
- **2 onions, finely sliced**
- **4 cups (1 liter) vegetable stock**
- **3/4 cup (200 ml) sour cream**
- **Cracked pepper**

**Serves: 4**
**Preparation: 10 minutes**
**Cooking: 15 minutes**
**Level: 1**

# ZUCCHINI SOUP



Heat the oil in a large saucepan over low heat. • Add the onions and garlic and sweat for 5 minutes. • Add the zucchini and stock and bring to a boil. • Simmer gently for 10 minutes. • Serve hot.

**1/4 cup (60 ml) extra-virgin olive oil**
**2 onions, finely sliced**
**3 cloves garlic, finely sliced**
**4 medium zucchini (courgettes), thinly sliced into rounds**
**4 cups (1 liter) vegetable stock**

Serves: 4
Preparation: 10 minutes
Cooking: 15 minutes
Level: 1

# TOMATO AND FENNEL SOUP

Trim the fennel, reserving a little of the leafy top leaves to garnish. • Finely slice one-third of the fennel bulbs and set aside. Coarsely chop the remainder. • Heat the butter in a large saucepan over low heat. • Add the coarsely chopped fennel and garlic and simmer for 10 minutes. • Increase the heat to medium-low and add the tomatoes. Simmer for 15 minutes, or until the tomatoes are soft and pulpy. • Purée with a hand-held blender or in a food processor. • Return to the heat and add the stock and finely sliced fennel. • Bring to a boil and simmer for 10 minutes, or until the fennel is tender. Garnish with the reserved fennel leaves and serve hot.

**2 medium fennel bulbs, with leafy tops**

**3 tablespoons (45 g) butter**

**3 cloves garlic, finely chopped**

**3 pounds (1.5 kg) plum (roma) tomatoes, peeled and quartered**

**3 cups (750 ml) vegetable stock**

**Serves: 4**
**Preparation: 15 minutes**
**Cooking: 40 minutes**
**Level: 1**

■ ■ ■ *Fresh tomatoes may be replaced with equal quantities of chopped canned tomatoes.*

# LEEK AND POTATO SOUP



Melt the butter in a large saucepan over low heat. • Add the leeks and sauté for 5 minutes, or until softened. • Add the potatoes and sauté for 5 minutes. • Add the stock and bring to a boil. • Simmer for 15 minutes, or until the potatoes are tender. • Purée with a hand-held blender or in a food processor. • Reheat the soup for 2–3 minutes, garnish with the chives, and serve hot.

- **1/3 cup (90 g) butter**
- **2 leeks, finely sliced**
- **4 large potatoes, peeled and coarsely chopped**
- **4 cups (1 liter) chicken stock**
- **2 tablespoons chopped fresh chives or sprigs of fresh, flat-leaf parsley to garnish**

**Serves: 4**
**Preparation: 15 minutes**
**Cooking: 30 minutes**
**Level: 1**

■ ■ ■ *This is a variation on vichyssoise, the classic French soup.*

# PARSNIP AND CUMIN SOUP

Heat the oil in a large saucepan over medium heat. Add the onions and cumin seeds and gently fry for 5 minutes. • Add the parsnips and chicken stock and bring to a boil. • Simmer for 15 minutes, or until the parsnips are tender. • Purée with a hand-held blender or in a food processor. • Reheat the soup for 2–3 minutes and serve hot.

**3 tablespoons (45 ml) extra-virgin olive oil**

**2 medium onions, finely sliced**

**1 tablespoon cumin seeds**

**8 medium parsnips, peeled and coarsely chopped**

**4 cups (1 liter) chicken stock**

Serves: 4
Preparation: 10 minutes
Cooking: 25 minutes
Level: 1

# SPLIT PEA SOUP

Cmbine all the ingredients in a large saucepan and bring to a boil. • Simmer gently for 1 hour. • Remove the hock, cut the meat from the bone, and cut into cubes. Set aside. • Purée the pea soup using a hand-held blender or in a food processor. • Return the meat to the soup and heat through. Serve hot.

- **2 cups (200 g) green split peas, rinsed**
- **1 ham hock**
- **1 large carrot, coarsely chopped**
- **2 medium onions, coarsely chopped**
- **4 cups (1 liter) chicken stock**

**Serves: 4**
**Preparation: 15 minutes**
**Cooking: 1 hour 10 minutes**
**Level: 1**

# CREAM OF MUSHROOM SOUP

Melt the butter in a large saucepan over low heat. • Simmer the mushrooms and thyme for 5 minutes. • Add the flour and stir for 2 minutes, or until smooth. • Gradually add the stock, stirring constantly to prevent lumps from forming. • Bring to a boil and simmer for 10 minutes. • Purée with a hand-held blender or in a food processor. • Reheat the soup for 2–3 minutes and serve hot.

- **1/4 cup (60 g) butter**
- **14 ounces (400 g) mushrooms, sliced**
- **1/3 cup (50 g) all-purpose (plain) flour**
- **5 cups (1.25 liters) chicken stock**
- **2 tablespoons finely chopped fresh thyme + extra sprigs to garnish**

Serves: 4
Preparation: 10 minutes
Cooking: 20 minutes
Level: 1

# ANISE MUSHROOM SOUP



Combine the stock, garlic, and star anise in a large saucepan over medium heat. Bring to a boil and simmer gently for 15 minutes. • Add the bok choy and mushrooms. • Simmer for 4–5 minutes. • Serve hot.

**5 cups (1.25 liters) chicken stock**
**2 cloves garlic, finely sliced**
**1 star anise**
**4 baby bok choy, quartered**
**1 pound (500 g) oyster mushrooms, halved**

Serves: 4
Preparation: 10 minutes
Cooking: 20 minutes
Level: 1

# CAULIFLOWER SOUP

Combine the cauliflower, onion, and stock in a large saucepan over medium heat and bring to a boil. • Simmer for 10 minutes, or until the cauliflower is soft. • Purée with a hand-held blender or in a food processor. • Return to the heat and add the cream. Season with pepper and simmer gently for 1–2 minutes. Serve hot.

- **2 pounds (1 kg) cauliflower, coarsely chopped**
- **2 onions, coarsely chopped**
- **4 cups (1 liter) chicken stock**
- **1 cup (250 ml) light (single) cream**
- **Freshly ground white pepper**

Serves: 4
Preparation: 10 minutes
Cooking: 15 minutes
Level: 1

# ROASTED GARLIC SOUP

Preheat the oven to 375° (190°C/gas 5). • Place the garlic bulbs in a small roasting pan and roast for 30 minutes, or until soft. • Squeeze the garlic out of its skin and place in a large saucepan. • Add the onion, potatoes, stock, and rosemary. Bring to a boil and simmer for 10 minutes, or until the potatoes are soft. • Pureé with a hand-held blender or in a food processor. • Reheat the soup for 2–3 minutes, garnish with the sprigs of rosemary, and serve hot.

**4 bulbs garlic**

**1 onion, finely sliced**

**3 medium potatoes, peeled and coarsely chopped**

**4 cups (1 liter) chicken stock**

**1 1/2 tablespoons finely chopped fresh rosemary + extra sprigs to garnish**

Serves: 4
Preparation: 15 minutes
Cooking: 45 minutes
Level: 1

# COCONUT SHRIMP SOUP

Combine the curry paste and 1 cup (250 ml) of the fish stock in a large saucepan over medium heat. • Bring to a boil and simmer for 5 minutes. • Add the remaining 3 cups (750 ml) of stock, coconut milk, and lime juice. • Gently simmer for 5 minutes, but do not boil. • Add the shrimp and cook for 3–5 minutes, until shrimp are cooked and have changed color. • Serve hot.

**1 teaspoon Thai green curry paste**
**4 cups (1 liter) fish stock**
**1 (14-ounce/400-ml) can coconut milk**
**1/4 cup (60 ml) freshly squeezed lime juice**
**16 large shrimp (green prawns), peeled and deveined**

Serves: 4
Preparation: 10 minutes
Cooking: 15–20 minutes
Level: 1

■ ■ ■ *Thai green curry paste is available in Asian markets or the Asian foods section of your local supermarket.*

# SPICY FISH SOUP

Combine the stock, chilies, and cherry tomatoes in a large saucepan over medium heat and bring to a boil. • Simmer for 10 minutes. • Add the fish and cilantro and simmer for 7 more minutes, or until the fish is white and cooked through. • Serve hot.

**5 cups (1.25 liters) fish stock**

**3 large fresh, red chilies, halved, seeded, and finely chopped**

**8 ounces (250 g) cherry tomatoes, halved**

**1 pound (500 g) firm white fish (bream, porgy, monkfish), diced into bite-size pieces**

**3 tablespoons finely chopped fresh cilantro (coriander) leaves**

Serves: 4
Preparation: 10 minutes
Cooking: 20 minutes
Level: 1

# MISO SOUP WITH SNOW PEAS

Combine the vegetable stock, miso paste, and carrot in a large saucepan over medium heat. • Bring to a boil and simmer very gently for 5 minutes. Do not boil again. • Add the snow peas and tofu and gently heat for 3 minutes. • Serve hot.

- **5 cups (1.25 liters) vegetable stock**
- **5 tablespoons miso**
- **1 carrot, julienned**
- **16 snow peas (sugar peas/mangetout), trimmed and finely sliced lengthwise**
- **14 ounces (400 g) soft silken tofu, diced**

Serves: 4
Preparation: 10 minutes
Cooking: 10 minutes
Level: 1

■ ■ ■ *Silken tofu has a soft, smooth texture and a high moisture content. Like all tofu (also known as bean curd and soybean curd), it is made from soy milk. Miso is a common ingredient in Japanese cooking, where it is used to thicken and flavor foods. Miso paste is available in several different varieties. They all work well in this recipe.*

# EGG DROP SOUP

Combine the stock and mushrooms in a large saucepan and bring to a boil. • Boil for about 15 minutes, or until the stock has reduced by one-third. • Add the leek and lemon juice. • Slowly pour in the eggs, whisking constantly, so that long strands form. • Serve hot.

**8** **cups (2 liters) chicken stock**

**12** **oyster mushrooms, thinly sliced**

**1** **leek, trimmed and cut into 3-inch (8-cm) matchsticks**

**2** **tablespoons freshly squeezed lemon juice**

**4** **large eggs, lightly beaten**

Serves: 4–6
Preparation: 5 minutes
Cooking: 15 minutes
Level: 1

# SALADS

# FRISÉE AND BACON SALAD

Slice the bacon into 1-inch (2.5-cm) strips. • Fry the bacon in a large frying pan over medium heat until crisp, then remove and set aside. • Fry the bread in the bacon fat until light golden brown and crisp. • Tear the frisée and transfer to a large bowl. • Peel and chop the eggs in half. • Add the eggs, bacon, bread, and vinegar to the lettuce. Toss gently and serve at once.

**8 slices bacon**

**2 cups cubed bread**

**1 large head frisée lettuce or curly endive, leaves separated**

**4 eggs, soft boiled**

**1/4 cup (60 ml) red wine or balsamic vinegar**

**Serves: 2–4**
**Preparation: 15 minutes**
**Cooking: 10 minutes**
**Level: 1**

■ ■ ■ *This salad is best if served when the ingredients are still slightly warm. To obtain soft boiled eggs, with the whites firm enought to cut and the yolks still moist, lower the eggs into a pan of salted, boiling water and simmer uncovered for 10 minutes. Immediately plunge the eggs into cold water.*

# GREEN BEAN AND ALMOND SALAD

Preheat the oven to 350°F (180°C/gas 4). • Spread out the almonds on a baking sheet and lightly roast for 5 minutes. • Cut the tops off the beans and steam until just tender, about 5 minutes. • Whisk the lemon juice and olive oil in a small bowl until well mixed. • Combine the beans, almonds, and beet greens in a large salad bowl. • Drizzle with the lemon dressing and toss well. • Serve at once.

**3/4 cup (120 g) salted almonds**

**1 pound (500 g) green beans**

**3 tablespoons (45 ml) freshly squeezed lemon juice**

**1/4 cup (60 ml) extra-virgin olive oil**

**3 cups baby beet (beetroot/red beet) greens**

**Serves: 4**
**Preparation: 10 minutes**
**Cooking: 10 minutes**
**Level: 1**

# SPINACH, GRAPEFRUIT, AND OLIVE SALAD

Combine the spinach, olives, and onion in a large salad bowl. • Peel and segment the grapefruit over a bowl to collect the juice that will drip as you work. Reserve for the dressing. Add the segments to the bowl. • Whisk the grapefruit juice and olive oil in a small bowl until well mixed. • Drizzle over the the salad and toss well. • Serve at once.

- **4 cups (200 g) baby spinach leaves**
- **1/2 cup (50 g) pitted (stoned) black olives**
- **1 small red onion, thinly sliced**
- **3 pink grapefruit**
- **1/3 cup (90 ml) extra-virgin olive oil**

**Serves: 4**
**Preparation: 20 minutes**
**Level: 1**

# PAPAYA AND WATERCRESS SALAD

Cut the papaya into quarters, remove the skin, and scoop out the seeds. • Slice into 3/4-inch (2-cm) thick pieces. • Combine the papaya and watercress in a large salad bowl. • Whisk the lime juice and sesame oil in a small bowl until well mixed. • Add the black sesame seeds and drizzle over the salad. • Toss well and serve at once.

- **1 large papaya**
- **3 cups watercress**
- **1/4 cup (60 ml) freshly squeezed lime juice**
- **2 tablespoons (30 ml) Asian sesame oil**
- **2 tablespoons black sesame seeds**

**Serves: 4**
**Preparation: 15 minutes**
**Level: 1**

■ ■ ■ *Papaya is a pear-shaped tropical fruit native to the Americas but now cultivated in hot climates around the world.*

# CANNELLINI BEAN AND ARTICHOKE SALAD

Halve the artichokes and put into a large salad bowl. • Add the cannellini beans and parsley. • Whisk the lemon juice and 1/4 cup (60 ml) of the artichoke oil in a small bowl until well mixed. • Drizzle over the bean mixture and season with salt to taste. Toss gently. • Serve at once.

**1 (12-ounce/300-g) jar marinated artichokes, oil reserved**

**1 (14-ounce/400-g) can cannellini beans, rinsed and drained**

**1 1/2 cups (150 g) fresh flatleaf parsley leaves**

**1/4 cup (60 ml) freshly squeezed lemon juice**

**Salt**

**Serves: 4**
**Preparation: 10 minutes**
**Level: 1**

# PROSCUITTO AND FIG SALAD

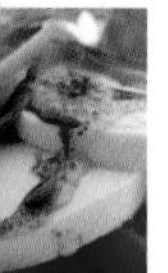



Whisk the balsamic vinegar and olive oil in a small bowl until well mixed. • Arrange the endive, figs, and prosciutto on four serving plates. • Drizzle with the balsamic dressing. Serve at once.

**5 tablespoons (75 ml) balsamic vinegar**
**1/4 cup (60 ml) extra-virgin olive oil**
**1 large head or 2 cups baby curly endive leaves**
**4 fresh figs, quartered**
**8 slices prosciutto**

**Serves: 4**
**Preparation: 10 minutes**
**Level: 1**

■ ■ ■ *If preferred, replace the prosciutto in this salad with eight large slices of salami.*

# WARM LENTIL SALAD

Preheat the oven to 350°F (180°C/gas 4). • Put the tomatoes on a baking sheet and drizzle with 1 tablespoon of the oil. Season with salt to taste. • Roast until softened, about 10 minutes. Remove and set aside. • Heat the remaining 3 tablespoons of oil in a medium saucepan over medium heat and add the lentils. • Cook until warmed through, about 5 minutes. • Combine the lentils and tomatoes, including any juices, in a large salad bowl. • Add the spinach leaves to the bowl and toss gently. The spinach should wilt a little. • Season with salt, if liked, and toss gently. • Serve at once.

**8 ounces (250 g) cherry tomatoes**
**1/4 cup (60 ml) extra-virgin olive oil**
**Salt**
**1 1/2 cups (400 g) cooked or canned brown lentils, rinsed and drained**
**3 cups (150 g) baby spinach leaves**

**Serves: 4**
**Preparation: 10 minutes**
**Cooking: 15 minutes**
**Level: 1**

# SWEET ROASTED VEGETABLE SALAD

Preheat the oven to 400°F (220°C/gas 6). • Place the bell peppers on a baking sheet. • Roast until the skins begin to blister, about 30 minutes. • Remove the bell peppers from the oven and place in a small bowl. • Cover with plastic wrap (cling film) and allow to cool for 10 minutes. • Remove the seeds and skins from bell peppers under running cold water. • Slice into strips. • Slice the sweet potatoes into 3/4-inch (2-cm) rounds. • Place on a baking sheet and drizzle with 1 tablespoon of the oil. • Roast until light brown and tender, about 15 minutes. • Combine the sweet potatoes, bell peppers, and arugula in a large salad bowl. • Add the remaining 3 tablespoons of oil and toss gently. • Divide the salad among four serving plates and top with the Parmesan. Serve at once.

**3** **red bell peppers (capsicums)**
**2** **large sweet potatoes, peeled**
**1/4** **cup (60 ml) extra-virgin olive oil**
**2** **cups (100 g) arugula (rocket) leaves, washed**
**1/2** **cup (60 g) Parmesan cheese, shaved**

**Serves: 4**
**Preparation: 25 minutes**
**Cooking: 45 minutes**
**Level: 1**

# ASIAN COLESLAW

Combine the cabbage, carrot, and mint in a large bowl. • Toss thoroughly. • Whisk the lime juice and soy sauce in a small bowl until well mixed. • Add to the cabbage mixture and toss well. • Serve at once.

- **3 cups (150 g) shredded Napa cabbage or Chinese cabbage (wombok)**
- **1 1/2 cups (75 g) grated carrot**
- **1/2 cup (25 g) coarsely chopped fresh mint**
- **5 tablespoons (75 ml) freshly squeezed lime juice**
- **3 tablespoons (45 ml) soy sauce**

**Serves: 4**
**Preparation: 15 minutes**
**Level: 1**

# GRILLED HALOUMI AND TOMATO SALAD

Slice the cheese into eight pieces.
• Cook in a large frying pan for 3 minutes on each side, or until golden brown.
• Combine the tomatoes, balsamic vinegar, and basil in a large bowl.
• Add the lettuce leaves and toss well.
• Arrange half the salad on four serving plates. Cover with slice of haloumi and top with the remaining salad.
• Serve at once.

**12 ounces (350 g) haloumi or feta cheese**

**12 cherry tomatoes, halved**

**1/3 cup (90 ml) balsamic vinegar**

**2 tablespoons finely chopped basil**

**3 cups (150 g) mixed lettuce leaves**

**Serves: 4**
**Preparation: 15 minutes**
**Cooking: 6 minutes**
**Level: 1**

# SMOKED CHICKEN AND MANGO SALAD

Preheat the oven to 350°F (180°C/gas 4). • Spread out the walnuts on a baking sheet and lightly roast for 5 minutes. • Slice the smoked chicken and put into in a large bowl. • Cut the mangoes into 3/4-inch (2-cm) cubes and add to the chicken. • Add the endive and walnuts to the chicken and toss well. • Add the vinegar and toss gently. Serve at once.

- **3/4 cup (90 g) walnuts**
- **3 smoked chicken breasts**
- **2 mangoes, peeled**
- **3 cups (150 g) curly endive leaves**
- **1/3 cup (90 ml) red wine vinegar**

**Serves: 4**
**Preparation: 15 minutes**
**Cooking: 5 minutes**
**Level: 1**

# PEPPERED PINEAPPLE SALAD

Slice the pineapple into 3/4-inch (2-cm) slices. • Combine the pineapple, arugula, and snow pea shoots in a large salad bowl. • Drizzle with the olive oil and toss gently. Season to taste with cracked pepper. Season with cracked pepper to taste. • Serve at once.

- **1 pineapple, peeled, quartered, and cored**
- **3 cups (150 g) arugula (rocket) leaves**
- **1 1/2 cups (150 g) snow pea (sugar pea/mangetout) shoots**
- **1/4 cups (60 ml) extra-virgin olive oil**
- **Cracked pepper**

**Serves: 4**
**Preparation: 15 minutes**
**Level: 1**

# ASPARAGUS AND POMEGRANATE SALAD

Bring a large saucepan of water to a boil over high heat. • Remove the woody ends from the asparagus and cut in half. • Blanch for 3 minutes, or until tender. • Refresh in cold water to stop the cooking process. • Divide the asparagus evenly among four serving plates. • Sprinkle the pomegranate seeds over the asparagus and place small lumps of goat cheese on top. • Drizzle with the balsamic vinegar. • Season with cracked pepper to taste. • Serve at once.

**32 asparagus spears**

**3/4 cup (180 g) soft goat cheese**

**1 pomegranate, seeded**

**1/3 cup (90 ml) balsamic vinegar**

**Cracked pepper**

Serves: 4
Preparation: 15 minutes
Cooking: 3 minutes
Level: 1

# ROASTED BEET SALAD WITH PRESERVED LEMON

Preheat the oven to 350°F (180°C/gas 4). • Place the beets in a roasting pan and drizzle with 1 tablespoon of oil. Cover with foil. • Roast, shaking the pan every 15 minutes, for 45–60 minutes, until tender. • Let cool and remove the skin. Cut in half or slice thickly, depending on the size of the beets. • Combine the beets, arugula, and preserved lemons in a large salad bowl. • Whisk the honey and remaining oil in a small bowl until well mixed. • Drizzle over the salad and toss well. • Serve at once.

- **12 baby beets (beetroot), trimmed**
- **1/3 cup (90 ml) extra-virgin olive oil**
- **3 cups arugula (rocket) leaves**
- **2 preserved lemons, flesh removed and zest thinly sliced**
- **3 tablespoons (45 ml) honey**

**Serves: 4**
**Preparation: 20 minutes**
**Cooking: 45–60 minutes**
**Level: 1**

■ ■ ■ *You can find preserved lemons wherever Middle Eastern foods are sold.*

# EGGPLANT AND BELL PEPPER SALAD WITH PESTO DRESSING



Preheat the oven to 400°F (200°C/gas 6) • Place the bell peppers on a baking sheet. • Roast for 30 minutes or until the skin begins to blister all over. • Remove the bell peppers from the oven and place in a small bowl. • Cover with plastic wrap (cling film) and allow to cool for 10 minutes. • Remove the seeds and skins from the bell peppers under running cold water. • Slice into quarters lengthwise. • Place the eggplants on a baking sheet skin side down. Roast for 15 minutes, or until soft. • Combine the eggplants, bell peppers, and spinach in a large bowl. • Whisk the pesto and lemon juice in a small bowl until well mixed. • Drizzle over the salad and toss well. • Serve at once.

- **4 red bell peppers (capsicums)**
- **8 baby eggplants (aubergine), halved lengthwise**
- **3 cups (150 g) baby spinach**
- **1/3 cup (90 g) pesto**
- **1/3 cup (90 ml) freshly squeezed lemon juice**

**Serves: 4**
**Preparation: 20 minutes**
**Cooking: 45 minutes**
**Level: 2**

# WATERCRESS SALAD WITH FENNEL AND PANCETTA

Preheat the oven to 350°F (180°C/gas 4). • Arrange the pancetta slices on a baking sheet in a single layer. Cook until crisp, about 8 minutes, then set aside. • Thinly slice the fennel lengthwise and put into in a large salad bowl. • Add the watercress and pancetta. • Peel and segment the oranges over a small bowl to collect the orange juice that drips as you work. Reserve for the dressing. Add the orange segments to the salad bowl. • Whisk the orange juice and oil in a small bowl until well mixed. • Drizzle over the salad and toss gently. • Serve at once.

**20 slices pancetta**
**3 bulbs baby fennel, halved, cored**
**3 cups (150 g) watercress**
**2 oranges**
**1/3 cup (90 ml) extra-virgin olive oil**

Serves: 4
Preparation: 20 minutes
Cooking: 8 minutes
Level: 1

■ ■ ■ *Watercress is native to Europe and Central Asia and is one of the oldest known leaf vegetables eaten by humans. It belongs to the cabbage family and is noted for its delicious peppery flavor. It makes a tasty base for a range of salads. Watercress is a good source of iron, calcium, and folic acid, as well as vitamins A and C. Many benefits from eating watercress are claimed—that it is a source of phytochemicals and antioxidants, a diuretic, and a digestive aid. It also appears to have cancer-suppressing properties and is believed to help defend against lung cancer.*

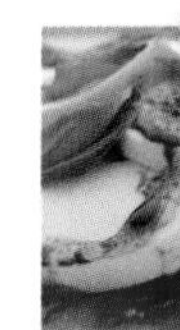

# BELGIAN ENDIVE AND BLUE CHEESE SALAD

Quarter the pears and remove the core. Slice each quarter into three and set aside. • Arrange the endives and pear slices on four serving plates. • Sprinkle with the cilantro and pieces of blue cheese. • Drizzle with the red wine vinegar. • Serve at once.

- **3 brown-skinned pears, such as Bosc, skinned**
- **3 heads Belgian endive (wiltof), leaves separated**
- **4 tablespoons fresh cilantro (coriander) leaves**
- **8 ounces (250 g) soft blue cheese**
- **1/3 cup (90 ml) red wine vinegar**

**Serves: 4**
**Preparation: 15 minutes**
**Level: 1**

■ ■ ■ *If you are not serving this salad immediately, drizzle the slices of pear with a little freshly squeezed lemon juice to prevent them from turning brown.*

# CUCUMBER, PEA, AND MINT SALAD

Bring a small saucepan of water to a boil over high heat. • Blanch the peas for 2 minutes. • Refresh in cold water to stop the cooking process. • Using a peeler, cut the cucumbers into ribbon lengths. • Combine the cucumbers, peas, arugula, mint, and orange zest in a large bowl. • Drizzle with the orange juice and toss well. • Serve at once.

**1 cup (150 g) frozen baby peas**
**2 cucumbers**
**4 cups (200 g) arugula (rocket) leaves**
**3/4 cup (40 g) fresh mint leaves**
**Zest and juice of 2 oranges**

Serves: 4
Preparation: 15 minutes
Cooking: 2 minutes
Level: 1

# AVOCADO AND ORANGE SALAD

Using a large spoon, scoop out the avocado flesh. • Dice into 3/4-inch (2-cm) pieces and put into a large bowl. • Add the watercress and pistachios. • Peel and segment the oranges over a bowl to collect the juice that drips as you work. Reserve for the dressing. Add the orange segments to the salad bowl. • Whisk the orange juice and olive oil in a small bowl until well mixed. • Drizzle over the salad and toss well. • Serve at once.

- **3 avocados, halved and pitted (stoned)**
- **3 cups (150 g) watercress sprigs**
- **3/4 cup (90 g) pistachios**
- **3 oranges**
- **1/3 cup (90 ml) extra-virgin olive oil**

**Serves: 4**
**Preparation: 20 minutes**
**Level: 1**

# TOASTED BREAD, PROSCUITTO, AND ASPARAGUS SALAD

Preheat the oven to 400°F (200°C/ gas 6). • Arrange the proscuitto on a baking sheet and bake until crisp, 10–15 minutes. • Set aside and reserve the fat. • Tear the bread into bite-sized pieces and put on a baking sheet. • Drizzle with the reserved fat and 1 tablespoon of oil, if necessary, to lightly coat each piece. • Bake for 15 minutes, or until crisp and golden brown. • Bring a large saucepan of salted water to a boil over high heat. • Blanch the asparagus for 3 minutes, or until tender. • Refresh in cold water to stop the cooking process. • Combine the asparagus, bread, and proscuitto in a large bowl. • Whisk the vinegar and remaining olive oil in a small bowl until well mixed. • Drizzle over the salad and toss well. • Serve at once.

**12 slices proscuitto**
**$^1/_2$ loaf olive bread, crust removed**
**32 asparagus spears, woody ends removed and halved**
**$^1/_3$ cup (90 ml) extra-virgin olive oil**
**$^1/_3$ cup (90 ml) sherry vinegar**

**Serves: 4**
**Preparation: 15 minutes**
**Cooking: 28–33 minutes**
**Level: 1**

# SMOKED TROUT SALAD

Bring a medium saucepan of water to a boil over high heat. • Blanch the snowpeas for 2 minutes. • Refresh in cold water to stop the cooking process. • Combine the snow peas, bean sprouts, cherry tomatoes, and raspberry vinegar in a large bowl. • Flake the trout into bite-sized pieces and add to salad. Gently mix and serve at once.

- **2 cups (150 g) snow peas (sugar peas/ magetout), trimmed and strings removed**
- **1 cup (50 g) bean sprouts**
- **1 pound (500 g) cherry tomatoes, halved**
- **1/3 cup (90 ml) raspberry vinegar**
- **1 smoked trout, halved and bones removed**

Serves: 4
Preparation: 15 minutes
Cooking: 2 minutes
Level: 1

# POTATO AND CRISP CHORIZO SALAD

Bring a large saucepan of water to a boil over high heat. • Cook the potatoes for 10 minutes, or until just tender. Drain. • Dry-fry the sausage in a large frying pan on high heat for 4 minutes, or until crisp. • Combine the potatoes, sausage, and radicchio in a large salad bowl. • Peel the eggs and cut in half and add to the salad. • Add the mayonnaise and stir carefully. • Serve at once.

- **1 pound (500 g) smooth skinned waxy potatoes, scrubbed, thickly sliced**
- **8 ounces (250 g) Spanish chorizo sausage, thinly sliced lengthwise**
- **1 head red radicchio, leaves separated**
- **4 eggs, soft-boiled (see note on page 148)**
- **3/4 cup (180 ml) mayonnaise**

**Serves: 4**
**Preparation: 10 minutes**
**Cooking: 15 minutes**
**Level: 1**

# RADICCHIO AND APPLE SALAD

Cut the apples into quarters and remove the cores. • Slice each quarter into three pieces and put into a large salad bowl. • Drizzle with the sherry vinegar and toss gently. • Add the pistachios, radicchio, and feta. • Toss gently and serve at once.

**2 crisp green apples (Granny Smiths are ideal)**
**1/3 cup (90 ml) sherry vinegar**
**1/2 cup (60 g) pistachios, roasted**
**2 small heads red radicchio, leaves separated**
**8 ounces (250 g) feta cheese, crumbled**

**Serves: 4**
**Preparation: 15 minutes**
**Level: 1**

# ORANGE, SNOW PEA, AND CASHEW SALAD

Bring a medium saucepan of water to a boil over high heat. • Blanch the snow peas for 2 minutes. • Refresh in cold water to stop the cooking process. • Combine the snow peas, spinach, and cashews in a large bowl. • Peel and segment the oranges over a bowl to collect the juice that drips as you work. Reserve for the dressing. Add the segments to the salad. • Whisk the orange juice and sesame oil in a small bowl until well mixed. • Drizzle over the salad and toss gently. • Serve at once.

- **1 1/2 cups (100 g) snow peas (sugar peas/ mangetout), trimmed**
- **3 cups (150 g) baby spinach leaves**
- **1/2 cup (80 g) salted cashew nuts, toasted**
- **2 oranges**
- **3 tablespoons (45 ml) Asian sesame oil**

**Serves: 4**
**Preparation: 12 minutes**
**Cooking: 2 minutes**
**Level: 1**

# NEW POTATO SALAD

Bring a large pot of salted water to a boil over high heat. • Boil the potatoes until tender, 10–15 minutes (depending on the size of the potatoes). • Combine the yogurt, horseradish cream, and olive oil in a large bowl. • Drain the potatoes and add to the yogurt dressing, mixing well. • Cut the chives into 1-inch (2.5-cm) lengths. Add to the potatoes and toss gently. • Serve at once.

- **2 pounds (1 kg) small new potatoes**
- **½ cup (125 g) plain yogurt**
- **¼ cup (60 ml) extra-virgin olive oil**
- **1 tablespoon horseradish cream**
- **1 bunch chives**

Serves: 4–6
Preparation: 10 minutes
Cooking: 10–15 minutes
Level: 1

# LEEK AND SEAWEED SALAD

Soak the wakame seaweed in cold water for 10 minutes, then remove the tough center rib. • Fill the bottom of a steamer with 2 inches (5 cm) of water. • Place over high heat and bring to a boil. • Cut the leeks in half and then in half lengthwise. • Slice the wakame into 1/2-inch (1-cm) wide pieces. Place the leeks in the top of the steamer and cook for 4 minutes. • Add the wakame for the last 30 seconds of cooking. • Transfer to a medium bowl. Mix in the sesame oil, vinegar, and sesame seeds. • Serve at once.

**8 (6-inch/15-cm) strips wakame seaweed**
**3 leeks**
**3 tablespoons (45 ml) apple-cider vinegar**
**2 tablespoons (30 ml) Asian sesame oil**
**2 tablespoons sesame seeds, toasted**

**Serves: 4**
**Preparation: 20 minutes**
**Cooking: 5 minutes**
**Level: 1**

■ ■ ■ *Wakame is a dark green seaweed with a mild flavor. In Japanese cuisine it is cooked and served like a green vegetable. It is available at health food stores and Asian markets.*

# ROMAINE AND WATERMELON SALAD

Place the lettuce a medium salad bowl.
• Add the watermelon to the lettuce.
• Whisk the vinegar and olive oil in a small bowl to make a dressing.
• Drizzle over the salad and toss well.
• Serve topped with cracked pepper.

**4 cups (200 g) torn hearts of romaine (cos) lettuce**
**2 cups (400 g) peeled and cubed watermelon**
**1/4 cup (60 ml) red wine vinegar**
**3 tablespoons (45 ml) extra-virgin olive oil**
**Cracked pepper, to taste**

Serves: 4
Preparation: 10 minutes
Level: 1

# MOZZARELLA, TOMATO, AND BASIL SALAD

Slice the mozzarella and tomatoes into 1/2-inch (1-cm) thick slices. • On four serving plates create layers of mozzarella and tomato. • Sprinkle the basil over the top. • Whisk the olive oil and balsamic vinegar together in a small bowl. • Drizzle over the salad. Serve at once.

- **8 ounces (250 g) fresh buffalo or cow's milk mozzarella**
- **8 large ripe tomatoes**
- **4 tablespoons finely chopped fresh basil**
- **1/4 cup (60 ml) extra-virgin olive oil**
- **1/3 cup (90 ml) balsamic vinegar**

**Serves: 4**
**Preparation: 15 minutes**
**Level: 1**

■ ■ ■ *This is a classic Italian salad. In its homeland it is known as a "caprese" after the beautiful island of Capri off the coast of Naples.*

# SMOKED SALMON AND CAPERBERRY SALAD

Whisk the lemon juice and olive oil together in a large bowl. • Add the caperberries and watercress and toss gently. • Arrange the salmon slices to make a circle in the center of four serving plates. • Place a small pile of the prepared salad in the center of the salmon. • Serve at once.

- **1/3 cup (90 ml) freshly squeezed lemon juice**
- **1/3 cup (90 ml) extra-virgin olive oil**
- **16 caperberries (see page 448)**
- **1 cup (100 g) watercress sprigs**
- **16 slices smoked salmon**

**Serves: 4**
**Preparation: 15 minutes**
**Level: 1**

# MANGO NOODLE SALAD

Place the noodles in a medium bowl, cover with boiling water, and soak for 5–10 minutes. • Drain and transfer to a large bowl. • Add the mangoes, cilantro, peanuts, and sweet chili sauce. • Toss well and serve at room temperature.

**14 ounces (400 g) dried rice stick noodles**

**2 mangoes, peeled and thinly sliced**

**3/4 cup (40 g) fresh cilantro (coriander) leaves**

**1/2 cup (80 g) roasted salted peanuts**

**1/2 cup (125 ml) Thai sweet chili sauce**

Serves: 4

Preparation: 10 minutes + 5-10 minutes to soak noodles

Level: 1

# LAMB SALAD WITH YOGURT

Heat the oil in a large frying pan over high heat. • Cook the lamb fillets for 4 minutes on each side for medium rare, or longer if desired. • Slice the tomatoes in half and combine with the arugula in a large bowl. • Slice the lamb and toss with the salad. • Divide the salad among four serving plates. Top each one with a dollop of yogurt. Serve warm.

- **3 tablespoons (45 ml) extra-virgin olive oil**
- **1 pound (500 g) lamb tenderloin, sliced**
- **8 ounces (250 g) cherry tomatoes**
- **3 cups (150 g) arugula (rocket) leaves**
- **3/4 cup (180 ml) plain Greek-style yogurt**

Serves: 4
Preparation: 10 minutes
Cooking: 10 minutes
Level: 1

■ ■ ■ *This hearty salad can be thrown together in no time and and makes a delicious low-carb meal. If liked, add a peeled cubed cucmber and a teaspoon of finely chopped fresh mint leaves to the yogurt.*

# CHICKEN WALDORF SALAD

Place a grill pan over medium-high heat. • Grill the chicken for 5 minutes on each side until cooked through. • Set aside and keep warm. • Slice the apple quarters into four and put in a large bowl. Add the watercress and walnuts and toss well. • Slice the chicken thinly and add to the salad. • Drizzle with the ranch dressing. • Serve at room temperature.

- **4 boneless, skinless chicken breasts**
- **2 red apples, cored and cut into quarters**
- **3 cups (150 g) watercress**
- **1/2 cup (60 g) walnuts, toasted**
- **1/2 cup (125 ml) ranch dressing**

Serves: 4
Preparation: 10 minutes
Cooking: 10 minutes
Level: 1

# EGG AND POTATO SALAD

Bring a large pot of water to a boil. • Add the potatoes and boil for 7–10 minutes until tender. • Drain and let cool completely. • Cook the eggs in a medium saucepan of barely simmering water for 6 minutes. • Drain and let cool completely. • Shell the eggs and cut in half lengthwise. • Mix the potatoes, eggs, walnuts, capers, and mayonnaise in a large bowl. • Chill for 1 hour and serve.

**2 pounds (1 kg) new potatoes, cut in half**
**6 large eggs**
**1 cup (125 g) walnuts, toasted**
**2 tablespoons salt-cured capers, rinsed**
**3/4 cup (180 ml) mayonnaise**

**Serves: 4**
**Preparation: 15 minutes + 1 hour to chill**
**Cooking: 13–16 minutes**
**Level: 1**

# NIÇOISE SALAD

Cook the eggs in a medium saucepan of barely simmering water for 6 minutes. • Drain and let cool completely. • Shell the eggs and cut into quarters. • Blanch the green beans in a large saucepan of boiling water for 2 minutes. • Drain and rinse in ice-cold water to stop the cooking process. • Transfer to a large bowl. • Mix in the tuna, olives, and eggs. • Mix the lemon juice and oil reserved from the tuna in a small bowl. • Pour the dressing over the salad and toss well. • Serve at room temperature.

**6 large eggs**
**8 ounces (250 g) green beans**
**2 cups (400 g) canned tuna in olive oil, with oil reserved**
**3/4 cup (80 g) black olives**
**1/3 cup (90 ml) freshly squeezed lemon juice**

**Serves: 4**
**Preparation: 10 minutes**
**Cooking: 8 minutes**
**Level: 1**

■ ■ ■ *There are many variations on this classic salad. Feel free to experiment, but always keep the basic mix of tuna and eggs.*

# GRAINS

# TOMATO AND BASIL RISOTTO



Combine the tomatoes and stock in a medium saucepan. Bring to a boil and decrease the heat to keep it warm. • Melt 2 tablespoons of the butter in a large, deep frying pan. • Add the rice and cook for 2 minutes, stirring constantly. • Gradually add the tomato stock, 1/2 cup (125 ml) at a time. Cook and stir until each addition has been absorbed and the rice is tender, 15–18 minutes. • Stir in the remaining 2 tablespoons of butter and chopped basil. Let stand for 5 minutes. • Garnish with the basil leaves and serve hot.

- **2 (16-ounce/500-g) cans chopped tomatoes, with juice**
- **3 cups (750 ml) vegetable stock**
- **1/4 cup (60 g) butter, cut up**
- **2 cups (400 g) risotto rice (Arborio, Carnaroli, Vialone nano)**
- **5 tablespoons coarsely chopped fresh basil, plus whole leaves to garnish**

**Serves: 4**
**Preparation: 10 minutes + 5 minutes to stand**
**Cooking: 25 minutes**
**Level: 1**

■ ■ ■ *Making risotto is easy, although it does require constant stirring during the cooking process so that the rice gradually releases its starches, and the risotto takes on its delicious, creamy consistency. The choice of rice is also important; if possible, always use an Italian superfino rice. We have suggested three of the best Italian risotto rices—Arborio, Carnaroli, and Vialone nano—which are all widely available in supermarkets and specialty food stores.*

# SPINACH AND GORGONZOLA RISOTTO

Cook the spinach in a large pot of boiling water over medium heat for 7–10 minutes, until tender. • Drain, squeezing out the excess water, and transfer to a food processor or blender. Process until smooth, then set aside. • Melt 2 tablespoons of the butter in a large, deep frying pan. • Add the rice and cook for 2 minutes, stirring constantly. • Gradually add the stock, 1/2 cup (125 ml) at a time. Cook and stir until each addition has been absorbed and the rice is tender, 15–18 minutes. • Mix in the puréed spinach and the remaining 2 tablespoons of butter. • Spoon the risotto into serving dishes and top with the Gorgonzola. Serve hot.

- **2 bunches spinach, tough stems removed**
- **1/4 cup (60 g) butter, cut up**
- **2 cups (400 g) risotto rice (Arborio, Carnaroli, Vialone nano)**
- **4 cups (1 liter) chicken stock, heated**
- **1/2 cup (125 g) Gorgonzola cheese or other soft blue cheese, cut into cubes**

**Serves: 4**
**Preparation: 5 minutes**
**Cooking: 25–30 minutes**
**Level: 1**

# SHRIMP AND SAFFRON RISOTTO

Combine the saffron and stock in a medium saucepan. Bring to a boil, then decrease the heat to keep it warm. • Melt 2 tablespoons of the butter in a large, deep frying pan. • Add the rice and cook for 2 minutes, stirring constantly. • Gradually add the saffron stock, 1/2 cup (125 ml) at a time, stirring until each addition has been absorbed. • Add the shrimp with the last 1/2 cup (125 ml) of stock. • Cook and stir until the rice is tender and the shrimp are pink and cooked. The whole process should take 15–18 minutes. • Stir in the remaining 2 tablespoons of butter and let stand for 5 minutes. Serve hot.

**1/4 teaspoon crumbled saffron threads**

**4 cups (1 liter) fish stock**

**1/4 cup (60 g) butter, cut up**

**2 cups (400 g) risotto rice (Arborio, Carnaroli, Vialone Nano)**

**20 raw medium shrimp (prawns), shelled and deveined**

Serves: 4
Preparation: 10 minutes + 5 minutes to stand
Cooking: 30 minutes
Level: 1

# CHICKEN AND ASPARAGUS RISOTTO

Sauté the chicken in 2 tablespoons of the butter in a large, deep frying pan for 5 minutes, or until the meat has lost its pink color. • Add the rice and cook for 2 minutes, stirring constantly. • Gradually add the stock, $\frac{1}{2}$ cup (125 ml) at a time, stirring until each addition has been absorbed. • Add the asparagus with the last $\frac{1}{2}$ cup (125 ml) of stock. • Cook and stir until the rice and asparagus are tender. The whole process should take 15–18 minutes. • Stir in the remaining butter and let stand for 5 minutes. • Serve hot.

- **2 boneless, skinless chicken breasts, cut into small pieces**
- **$\frac{1}{3}$ cup (90 g) butter, cut up**
- **2 cups (400 g) risotto rice (Arborio, Carnaroli, Vialone nano)**
- **4 cups (1 liter) chicken stock, heated**
- **8 ounces (250 g) asparagus, woody ends removed and cut into short lengths**

**Serves: 4**
**Preparation: 10 minutes + 5 minutes to stand**
**Cooking: 25 minutes**
**Level: 1**

# FRIED RICE WITH EGG

Bring a large saucepan of salted water to a boil. • Add the rice and cook over medium heat for 10–15 minutes, until tender. • Drain well and set aside. • Cook the mushrooms in a large nonstick frying pan over medium heat for 5 minutes, until lightly browned. • Add the rice, scallions, and soy sauce. Cook, stirring, for 4 minutes. • Set aside and keep warm. • Fry the eggs in a large nonstick frying pan over medium heat for 3 minutes. • Arrange the fried rice on individual serving plates and top with the fried eggs. • Serve hot.

- **2 cups (400 g) basmati rice**
- **1 pound (500 g) button mushrooms, thinly sliced**
- **4 scallions (spring onions), thinly sliced**
- **1/3 cup (90 ml) soy sauce**
- **4 large eggs**

**Serves: 4**
**Preparation: 10 minutes**
**Cooking: 22–27 minutes**
**Level: 1**

# SAVORY RICE

Bring a large saucepan of salted water to a boil. • Add the rice and cook over medium heat for 10–15 minutes, until tender. • Drain well and set aside. • Cook the green beans in a small saucepan of boiling water for 4 minutes. • Drain and set aside. • Dry-fry the pancetta in a large frying pan over medium heat for 5 minutes. • Add the garlic and cook for 1 minute. • Add the green beans and rice. • Cook, stirring often, for 5 minutes, until heated through. • Add the eggs and serve hot.

**2 cups (400 g) basmati rice**

**12 ounces (350 g) green beans, trimmed**

**1¼ cups (150 g) diced pancetta**

**2 cloves garlic, finely chopped**

**6 hard-boiled eggs, shells removed and cut into quarters**

Serves: 4
Preparation: 15 minutes
Cooking: 25–30 minutes
Level: 1

# FRUITY WILD RICE

Bring a large saucepan of water to a boil. • Add the rice and cook over medium heat for about 40 minutes, or until tender. • Drain well. • Grate the zest from the oranges into a large bowl. • Peel and segment the oranges, catching any drips. Place the segments, and any juice, in the bowl with the zest. • Mix in the cooked rice, apricots, pistachios, and cilantro. • Serve hot.

- **2 cups (400 g) wild rice**
- **2 oranges**
- **1/4 cup (135 g) chopped dried apricots**
- **1/2 cup (80 g) salted pistachio nuts, toasted**
- **3 tablespoons finely chopped fresh cilantro (coriander)**

Serves: 4
Preparation: 15 minutes
Cooking: 40 minutes
Level: 1

# WILD RICE WITH ROASTED PEPPERS AND RAISINS

Bring a large saucepan of salted water to a boil. • Add the rice and cook over medium heat for about 40 minutes, or until tender. • Drain well. • Broil (grill) the bell peppers until the skins are blackened all over. • Wrap in a paper bag for 5 minutes, then remove the skins and seeds. Slice into strips. • Mix the bell peppers, golden raisins, onion, and five-spice powder in a large frying pan and stir over medium heat for 3 minutes. • Add the mixture to the cooked rice and mix well. Serve hot.

**2 cups (400 g) wild rice**
**2 red bell peppers (capsicums)**
**1/2 cup (90 g) golden raisins (sultanas)**
**1 large red onion, finely sliced**
**2 teaspoons five-spice powder**

Serves: 4
Preparation: 25 minutes + 5 minutes to stand
Cooking: 45 minutes
Level: 2

# FRAGRANT JASMINE RICE WITH ASIAN HERBS

Bring a large saucepan of salted water to a boil. • Add the rice and cook over medium heat for 10–15 minutes, until tender. • Drain well. • Mix the cilantro, basil, mint, and lime zest and juice in a large bowl. • Add the rice and stir until well mixed. Serve hot.

**2 cups (400 g) jasmine rice**

**3 tablespoons fresh cilantro (coriander) leaves**

**2 tablespoons holy basil, Thai basil, or other basil leaves**

**2 tablespoons Vietnamese or other mint leaves**

**Finely grated zest and juice of 2 limes**

Serves: 4
Preparation: 5 minutes
Cooking: 10–15 minutes
Level: 1

# COCONUT RICE

Mix the rice, coconut milk, and 2⅔ cups (400 ml) salted water in a medium saucepan. • Bring to a boil and simmer over low heat for 15–20 minutes, until the rice is cooked and all the liquid has been absorbed. • Remove from the heat and mix in the peanuts and cilantro. Season with cracked peper to taste. • Let rest for 5 minutes. • Fluff the rice with a fork and serve hot.

- **2 cups (400 g) basmati rice**
- **1¼ cups (310 ml) coconut milk**
- **¾ cup (120 g) salted peanuts, toasted**
- **4 tablespoons fresh cilantro (coriander) leaves**
- **Cracked pepper**

**Serves: 4**
**Preparation: 5 minutes + 5 minutes to rest**
**Cooking: 15–20 minutes**
**Level: 1**

# CHORIZO AND BELL PEPPER PAELLA

Preheat the oven to 400°F (200°C/ gas 6). • Dry-fry the chorizo in a paella pan or large frying pan over medium heat for 3 minutes, until crisp. • Add the bell peppers and rice. Cook for 3 minutes, stirring constantly. • Pour in the stock and lemon zest and juice and bring to a boil. • Continue cooking over medium-high heat until all the liquid has almost been absorbed, about 10 minutes. The rice grains should still be slightly crunchy, but there should still be liquid in the pan. • Bake, uncovered, for 10 minutes. • Cover the pan with aluminum foil or parchment paper and let stand for 10 minutes before serving. • Garnish with the lemon wedges.

**5 ounces (150 g) Spanish chorizo sausage, thinly sliced**
**2 red bell peppers (capsicums), seeded and diced**
**2 cups (400 g) paella or short-grain rice**
**4 cups (1 liter) chicken stock, heated**
**Grated zest and juice of 2 lemons, plus lemon wedges to garnish**

Serves: 4
Preparation: 10 minutes + 10 minutes to stand
Cooking: 30 minutes
Level: 1

# STUFFED ZUCCHINI FLOWERS

Soak the zucchini flowers in ice-cold water for 2–3 minutes to make them open up. • Drain and set aside. • Mix the rice, tomatoes, and mint in a small bowl. • Stuff the zucchini flowers with the rice mixture. Do not overfill them as the rice will expand when it is cooked and the flowers may split. • Fold over the ends of the zucchini flowers to seal in the filling. • Lay the stuffed flowers in a large saucepan. Make two layers, if necessary, and ensure they are not too tightly packed. • Cover with the stock. • Place a plate upside down on top of the flowers to prevent them from floating. • Simmer for about 40 minutes, or until the rice is cooked. • Serve hot or at room temperature.

**20** **zucchini (courgette) flowers, cleaned**

**1/2** **cup (100 g) long-grain white rice**

**3** **tomatoes, peeled and coarsely chopped**

**3** **tablespoons finely chopped fresh mint**

**5** **cups (1.25 liters) chicken stock, heated**

**Serves: 4–6**
**Preparation: 20 minutes**
**Cooking: 40 minutes**
**Level: 2**

# SPICY CHICKEN FRIED RICE

Bring a large saucepan of salted water to a boil. • Add the rice and cook over medium heat for 10–15 minutes, until tender. • Drain well and set aside. • Heat $1\frac{1}{2}$ teaspoons of chili paste in a nonstick frying pan. Pour in the beaten eggs. • When the bottom is just set, side a wooden spatula under the eggs to loosen them from the pan. Shake the pan with a rotating movement to spread. • Cook until nicely browned on the underside and the top is set. • Remove from the heat and slice into strips. • Fry the chicken with the remaining chili paste in the same frying pan for 5 minutes, until the chicken is cooked. • Add the rice and cook for 4 minutes, until heated through. • Mix in the egg strips and scallions. • Serve hot.

**2 cups (400 g) basmati rice**
**2 tablespoons mild or spicy Thai red chili paste**
**3 eggs, lightly beaten**
**8 ounces (250 g) boneless, skinless chicken breasts or thighs, cut into small pieces**
**4 scallions (spring onions), sliced on the diagonal**

**Serves: 4**
**Preparation: 10 minutes**
**Cooking: 25–30 minutes**
**Level: 2**

# ONIGIRI

Put the rice in a medium saucepan and cover with 3/4 inch (2 cm) cold water. Bring to a boil, stirring to separate the grains. • Cover and decrease the heat to very low. • Cook for 20 minutes, until the rice is tender. • Drain well and use a fork to fluff the rice. • Mix the salmon and wasabi in a small bowl and set aside. • Fill a separate small bowl with cold water in which to dip your hands to prevent the rice from sticking. • Shape the rice into balls the size of golf balls. • Make a hollow in the center and fill with 1/2 teaspoon of the salmon mixture. • Form another ball the same size and place on top, then mold them together. • Flatten the balls and shape them into a triangle, about 1 inch (2.5 cm) thick and 3 inches (8 cm) high. • Wrap strips of nori under the bases of the rice triangles, smoothing them evenly up the sides. • Serve with soy sauce for dipping.

**2 cups (400 g) short- or medium-grain rice**

**3 ounces (90 g) smoked salmon slices, finely chopped**

**1 teaspoon wasabi paste**

**1 nori sheet, cut into 1 x 3-inch (2.5 x 8-cm) strips**

**1/2 cup (125 ml) soy sauce, for dipping**

**Serves: 2–4**
**Preparation: 20 minutes**
**Cooking: 20 minutes**
**Level: 2**

■ ■ ■ *Rice is one of our oldest food crops and is a staple food for half the population of the world. There are thousands of different types of rice, although most can be divided into three large groups—short-grain rice, medium-grain rice, and long-grain rice. Brown rice is the same as white rice but it still has its outer husk. It is richer in fiber and B vitamins than the more refined white rice.*

# MUSHROOM INARIS

Combine the rice and $2\frac{1}{2}$ cups (625 ml) of salted water in a medium saucepan. • Bring to a boil, decrease the heat, and simmer over low heat for 5 minutes. • Remove from the heat. Cover and let stand for 15 minutes until all the liquid has been absorbed. • Transfer the rice to a large bowl and mix in the rice wine vinegar. Let cool slightly. • Combine the mushrooms and 3 tablespoons of the soy sauce in a medium frying pan. • Cook over medium heat for 3–4 minutes, until softened. • Stir the mushroom and soy sauce mixture into the rice. • Tightly pack the tofu skins with the rice mixture and top each with a mushroom slice. • Serve with the remaining soy sauce for dipping.

■ ■ ■ *Dried bean curd, or tofu skins, is a Chinese and Japanese soybean product that is available from many ethnic food suppliers and at Asian food markets.*

- **2 cups (400 g) short-grain white rice**
- **$\frac{1}{4}$ cup (60 ml) rice wine vinegar**
- **24 shiitake mushroom caps, thinly sliced**
- **$\frac{1}{2}$ cup (125 ml) soy sauce**
- **12 dried tofu skins**

**Serves: 6**
**Preparation: 15 minutes + 15 minutes to stand**
**Cooking: 10 minutes**
**Level: 1**

# UMEBOSHI PLUM RICE BALLS

Mix the cooked rice, basil, and 3 tablespoons of the soy sauce in a large bowl until the rice becomes sticky. • Use your hands to roll the mixture into egg-sized balls. • Make a hollow in the center of each ball and add 1 teaspoon umeboshi purée. Close up the balls to seal in the filling. • Heat the oil in a deep-fryer or deep frying pan until very hot. • Fry the balls in small batches for 4–5 minutes, until golden brown. • Drain well on paper towels. Serve hot with the remaining soy sauce for dipping.

**3 cups (300 g) cooked brown rice**
**3 tablespoons finely chopped fresh holy basil, Thai basil, or other basil**
**3/4 cup (180 ml) soy sauce**
**8 umeboshi plums, pitted and puréed**
**2 cups (500 ml) vegetable oil**

Serves: 4
Preparation: 20 minutes
Cooking: 15 minutes
Level: 2

■ ■ ■ *Umeboshi are Japanese pickled plums and can be purchased wherever Japanese foods are sold. They are also available in a paste form. Chinese preserved plums can be substituted.*

# SWEET POTATO AND HERB MILLET



Combine the millet and stock in a large saucepan. Cover and bring to a boil. • Decrease the heat and simmer for 20 minutes. • Add the sweet potatoes and simmer for 15–20 minutes, until the millet and sweet potatoes are tender. • Stir in the sage and thyme. • Serve hot.

- **2 cups (400 g) millet**
- **5 cups (1.25 liters) chicken stock**
- **2 sweet potatoes, peeled and cut into 1/2-inch (1-cm) dice**
- **1 tablespoon finely chopped fresh sage**
- **1 tablespoon finely chopped fresh thyme**

Serves: 4
Preparation: 5 minutes
Cooking: 35–40 minutes
Level: 1

■ ■ ■ *Millet is a golden grain that resembles couscous and is a staple food in parts of Asia and Africa. It is an excellent source of B vitamins.*

# POLISH-STYLE BUCKWHEAT

Sauté the onion in the oil in a large saucepan over medium heat for 2 minutes. • Add the buckwheat and toast for 2 minutes. • Pour in the egg and stir quickly until the egg is cooked and the grains are separate. • Meanwhile, heat the stock in a separate large pot. Bring to a boil and pour over the buckwheat. • Simmer, uncovered, over low heat for 10 minutes, or until tender. • Fluff the grains lightly with a fork and serve hot.

**1** **large onion, thinly sliced**

**3** **tablespoons extra-virgin olive oil**

**2** **cups (400 g) roasted buckwheat groats or kasha**

**2** **eggs, lightly beaten**

**5** **cups (1.25 liters) vegetable stock**

**Serves: 4**
**Preparation: 5 minutes**
**Cooking: 15 minutes**
**Level: 1**

■ ■ ■ *Buckwheat groats, also known as kasha, are hulled buckwheat grains. They are sold both roasted and unroasted; unroasted kasha is pale and bland in flavor while the roasted grains are dark with a lovely earthy flavor.*

# QUINOA WITH GRAPEFRUIT

Bring the stock to a boil in a medium saucepan. • Decrease the heat to low and stir in the quinoa. • Cover and simmer for 15–20 minutes, until all the liquid has been absorbed. • Remove from the heat and set aside, covered. • Peel the grapefruits and break into segments. • Fluff the quinoa with a fork. • Mix the quinoa, golden raisins, chives, and grapefruit segments in a large bowl. • Serve hot.

- **4 cups (1 liter) vegetable stock**
- **2 cups (400 g) quinoa, rinsed**
- **3 grapefruits**
- **3/4 cup (135 g) golden raisins (sultanas)**
- **2 tablespoons chives, cut into short lengths**

**Serves: 4**
**Preparation: 10 minutes**
**Cooking: 15–20 minutes**
**Level: 1**

■ ■ ■ *This South American grain was the staple food of the Incas. Pronounced* keen-wa, *this light grain is an excellent source of plant protein, iron, potassium, magnesium, and lysine.*

# QUINOA WITH BRUSSELS SPROUTS

Bring the stock to a boil in a medium saucepan. • Decrease the heat to low and stir in the quinoa. • Cover and simmer for 10 minutes. • Add the Brussels sprouts and simmer for 5–10 minutes, until all the liquid has been absorbed and the sprouts are tender. • Stir in the walnuts and red onion. • Fluff the quinoa with a fork and serve hot.

- **2 cups (500 ml) chicken stock**
- **2 cups (400 g) quinoa, rinsed**
- **8 Brussels sprouts, thickly sliced**
- **3/4 cup (90 g) walnuts, toasted**
- **1 red onion, thinly sliced**

Serves: 4
Preparation: 10 minutes
Cooking: 15–20 minutes
Level: 1

# PEARL BARLEY PILAF

Combine the barley, stock, and oil in a large saucepan. Bring to a boil. • Cover and simmer over low heat for 30 minutes, until the barley is tender and all the liquid has been absorbed. • Remove from the heat. • Strip the leaves from the cilantro and parsley stems. Discard the stems. Mix in the cilantro and parsley leaves. • Serve hot.

- **2 cups (400 g) pearl barley**
- **6 cups (1.5 liters) chicken stock**
- **1/3 cup (90 ml) extra-virgin olive oil**
- **1 small bunch fresh cilantro (coriander)**
- **1 small bunch fresh parsley**

Serves: 4
Preparation: 10 minutes
Cooking: 30 minutes
Level: 1

■ ■ ■ *Deliciously chewy pearl barley makes a good base for a salad or it can be instead of rice.*

# BARLEY WITH PANCETTA AND FAVA BEANS

Dry-fry the pancetta in a large saucepan over medium heat for 3 minutes, until crisp. • Add the barley, fava beans, and garlic. Pour in the chicken stock. Bring to a boil. • Cover and simmer over low heat for 30 minutes, until the barley is tender and all the liquid has been absorbed. • Serve hot.

- **5 ounces (150 g) pancetta, diced**
- **$1^1/_2$ cups (300 g) pearl barley**
- **1 cup (100 g) frozen baby fava (broad) beans (or substitute frozen baby lima beans)**
- **2 cloves garlic, finely chopped**
- **4 cups (1 liter) chicken stock**

Serves: 4
Preparation: 5 minutes
Cooking: 35 minutes
Level: 1

# SPICED CURRANT COUSCOUS

Melt the butter in a medium saucepan. • Add the currants and garam masala. Cook over medium heat for 3 minutes. • Pour in the stock and bring to a boil. • Stir in the couscous. Cover and remove from the heat. • Let stand for 10 minutes, until the couscous has completely absorbed the liquid. • Fluff the couscous with a fork. Serve.

**1 tablespoon butter**
**1/2 cup (90 g) currants**
**2 teaspoons garam masala**
**2 cups (500 ml) vegetable stock**
**2 cups (400 g) instant couscous**

**Serves: 4**
**Preparation: 5 minutes + 10 minutes to stand**
**Cooking: 5 minutes**
**Level: 1**

■ ■ ■ *Although couscous is treated like a grain, it is actually a small granular pasta made of semolina. Quick and easy to prepare, couscous has become a staple on tables around the world.*

# ORANGE AND ALMOND COUSCOUS

Bring the orange juice to a boil in a small saucepan. • Mix the couscous, currants, and almonds in a medium bowl. • Pour the hot orange juice over the couscous mixture. • Cover the bowl with plastic wrap (cling film) and let stand for 10 minutes, until the couscous has completely absorbed the liquid. • Stir in the butter with a fork until melted. Serve hot.

**2 cups (500 ml) freshly squeezed orange juice**
**2 cups (400 g) instant couscous**
**$^3/_4$ cup (135 g) currants**
**1 cup (150 g) whole salted almonds, toasted**
**$^1/_4$ cup (60 g) butter, cut up**

Serves: 4
Preparation: 5 minutes + 10 minutes to stand
Cooking: 5 minutes
Level: 1

# STUFFED MINI PUMPKINS

Cut the top off each pumpkin and scoop out the seeds and fibers. Set the tops aside. • Dry-fry the bacon in a medium frying pan for 5 minutes, until crisp. • Set aside. • Bring the stock to a boil in a small saucepan. • Put the couscous in a medium bowl and pour in the hot stock. • Cover and let stand for 10 minutes, until the couscous has completely absorbed the liquid. • Mix in the bacon and pine nuts. • Fill the pumpkins with the couscous mixture and replace the pumpkin tops. • Line a large steamer with parchment paper, making holes in it so that the steam can come through. • Place the pumpkins on top of the paper and cover with a lid. • Place the steamer over a saucepan of boiling water. • Steam the pumpkins for 35–40 minutes, until they are tender. • Remove the lid and pumpkin tops. Fluff the couscous with a fork, replace the pumpkin tops, and serve hot.

- **4 Golden Nugget or other mini pumpkins, each weighing about 1¼-pound (600-g)**
- **6 slices bacon, coarsely chopped**
- **1½ cups (375 ml) chicken stock**
- **1½ cups (300 g) instant couscous**
- **½ cup (90 g) pine nuts, toasted**

**Serves: 4**
**Preparation: 20 minutes + 10 minutes to stand**
**Cooking: 40–45 minutes**
**Level: 2**

# ISRAELI COUSCOUS WITH DATES

Bring the orange juice to a boil in a small saucepan. • Pour the hot orange juice over the couscous in a large bowl. • Cover the bowl with plastic wrap (cling film) and let stand for 10 minutes, until the couscous has completely absorbed the liquid. • Mix in the dates, mint, and hazelnuts. • Fluff the couscous with a fork. Serve hot.

- **2 cups (500 ml) freshly squeezed orange juice**
- **2 cups (400 g) Israeli (large) couscous**
- **1 cup (180 g) dates, halved and pitted (stoned)**
- **4 tablespoons fresh mint leaves**
- **1 cup (150 g) salted hazelnuts, toasted and coarsely chopped**

Serves: 4
Preparation: 10 minutes + 10 minutes to stand
Cooking: 5 minutes
Level: 1

■ ■ ■ *Israeli couscous, also known as maftoul or pearly couscous, is a larger version of traditional couscous. It is made of a toasted mixture of bulgur and flour.*

# STUFFED EGGPLANT

Broil (grill) the bell pepper until the skin has blackened all over. • Wrap it in a paper bag for 5 minutes, then remove the skin and seeds. Slice into strips. • Put the bulgur in a small bowl and cover with hot water. • Let stand for 30 minutes. • Preheat the oven to 375°F (190°C/gas 5). • Halve the eggplants lengthwise. Use a sharp knife to hollow out the flesh, taking care not to pierce the skins. Dice the eggplant flesh and place it in a medium bowl. Reserve the shells. • Drain the bulgur well and add to the eggplant flesh with the bell pepper, walnuts, and goat cheese. • Spoon the mixture into the eggplant shells. • Arrange the stuffed eggplant halves in a baking dish. • Bake for 25–30 minutes, until the eggplants are cooked and the cheese has melted. • Serve hot.

**1 red bell pepper (capsicum)**

**1/2 cup (150 g) bulgur (cracked wheat)**

**2 medium eggplants (aubergines)**

**1/2 cup (50 g) coarsely chopped walnuts, toasted**

**4 ounces (125 g) goat cheese, cut up**

Serves: 2–4
Preparation: 20 minutes + 30 minutes to stand
Cooking: 30–35 minutes
Level: 2

# SYRIAN-STYLE BULGUR

Put the bulgur in a large bowl and cover with the hot chicken stock. • Let stand for 30 minutes. • Drain well. • Mix in the red cabbage, mint, and pomegranate seeds. • Serve hot.

- **2 cups (400 g) bulgur wheat (cracked wheat)**
- **4 cups (1 liter) chicken stock, hot**
- **2 cups (150 g) shredded red cabbage**
- **3 tablespoons coarsely chopped fresh mint**
- **Seeds from 1 pomegranate**

Serves: 4
Preparation: 5 minutes + 30 minutes to stand
Level: 1

■ ■ ■ *Bulgur is wheat that has been steamed whole, then dried and cracked into grits. The steaming process involved in its preparation means that bulgur is precooked and easy to prepare.*

# BAKED POLENTA

Bring the stock to a boil in a medium saucepan. • Gradually sprinkle in the polenta, stirring constantly with a wooden spoon to prevent lumps from forming. • Continue cooking over medium heat, stirring almost constantly, for about 15 minutes, or until the polenta is thick and starts to pull away from the sides of the pan. • Remove from the heat. • Stir in the sun-dried tomatoes, 3/4 cup (90 g) of the Parmesan, and basil. • Pour the mixture into a 12-inch (30-cm) nonstick springform pan. • Spread the mixture evenly, pressing it down with the back of a spoon. • Let cool for 10 minutes. • Loosen and remove the pan sides and sprinkle with the remaining 3 tablespoons of Parmesan. • Broil (grill) for 5 minutes, until warmed through. • Slice into wedges and serve.

**4 cups (1 liter) chicken stock**

**1 cup (150 g) instant polenta**

**1 cup (150 g) sun-dried tomatoes, finely chopped**

**3/4 cup (90 g) + 3 tablespoons freshly grated Parmesan cheese**

**3 tablespoons finely chopped fresh basil**

Serves: 4–6
Preparation: 10 minutes + 10 minutes to cool
Cooking: 20 minutes
Level: 2

# MUSHROOM POLENTA

Preheat the oven to 350°F (180°C/gas 4). • Place the mushrooms in a large baking dish. • Bake for 20 minutes, until softened. • Slice the mushrooms thickly and set aside. • Strip the leaves from the arugula stems. Set the leaves aside and discard the stems. • Bring the stock to a boil in a medium saucepan. • Gradually sprinkle in the cornmeal, stirring constantly with a wooden spoon to prevent lumps from forming. • Continue cooking over medium heat, stirring almost constantly, for 45–50 minutes, or until the polenta is thick and starts to pull away from the sides of the pan. • Remove from the heat. • Stir in the Parmesan. • Spoon the polenta into individual serving dishes. • Top with the mushrooms and arugula. • Serve hot.

- **8 large wild or portobello mushrooms**
- **1 small bunch arugula (rocket)**
- **8 cups (2 liters) vegetable stock**
- **2 cups (350 g) coarse-grain yellow cornmeal**
- **1 cup (125 g) freshly grated Parmesan cheese**

**Serves: 4**
**Preparation: 5 minutes**
**Cooking: 1 hour 5–10 minutes**
**Level: 2**

# PASTA

# RIGATONI WITH PEAS AND CRISPY BACON

Cook the rigatoni in a large pot of salted boiling water until al dente. • Dry-fry the bacon in a medium frying pan over medium heat for 3 minutes, until crispy. • Remove from the pan with a slotted spoon. • Add the garlic to the pan and sauté until pale gold. • Add the lemon zest and juice and peas. Cook for 2 minutes. • Drain the rigatoni and mix in the bacon, garlic, lemon zest and juice, and peas. • Toss well and serve hot.

- **1 pound (500 g) dried rigatoni**
- **8 slices bacon, cut into thin strips**
- **4 cloves garlic, thinly sliced**
- **Finely grated zest and juice of 2 lemons**
- **2 cups (250 g) fresh or frozen and thawed peas**

**Serves: 4**
**Preparation: 10 minutes**
**Cooking: 12 minutes**
**Level: 1**

# TORTELLINI WITH CREAMY MUSHROOM SAUCE



Cook the tortellini in a large pot of salted boiling water until al dente. • Combine the mushrooms, garlic, and 1/2 cup (125 ml) of the cream in a large frying pan over medium heat and cook for about 3 minutes, or until the mushrooms have softened and the cream has reduced by half. • Stir in the remaining 3/4 cup (180 ml) cream and Parmesan and simmer over low heat for 2 minutes. • Remove from the heat. • Drain the tortellini and add to the pan with the mushroom sauce. • Toss gently and serve hot.

**1 pound (500 g) meat-filled tortellini**
**10 ounces (300 g) mushrooms, thinly sliced**
**2 cloves garlic, finely chopped**
**1 1/4 cups (300 ml) light (single) cream**
**1/2 cup (60 g) freshly grated Parmesan cheese**

Serves: 4
Preparation: 10 minutes
Cooking: 10 minutes
Level: 1

# SPAGHETTI WITH ANCHOVIES AND BLACK OLIVES

Cook the spaghetti in a large pot of salted boiling water until al dente. • Sauté the anchovies and olives in the oil in a large frying pan over medium heat for 3 minutes. • Add the parsley and cook for 2 minutes. • Remove from the heat. • Drain the spaghetti and add to the pan with the anchovies. • Toss well and serve hot.

**1 pound (500 g) dried spaghetti**
**16 anchovies, cleaned and cut in half lengthwise**
**1 cup (100 g) pitted (stoned) black olives**
**1/4 cup (60 ml) extra-virgin olive oil**
**1 cup (50 g) coarsely chopped fresh parsley**

Serves: 4
Preparation: 5 minutes
Cooking: 15 minutes
Level: 1

# SPINACH AND RICOTTA CANNELLONI WITH TOMATO SAUCE

Preheat the oven to 350°F (180°C/gas 4). • Cook the spinach in a large pot of boiling water for 1 minute. • Drain well. • Coarsely chop the spinach and place in a large bowl. • Mix in the ricotta and nutmeg until well combined. • Use a pastry bag fitted with a 1/2-inch (1-cm) tip to fill the cannelloni tubes with the spinach and ricotta mixture. • Arrange the filled cannelloni in a shallow baking dish and pour the tomatoes over the top. • Bake, uncovered, for about 40 minutes, or until the pasta is al dente. • Serve hot.

**2 pounds (1 kg) spinach leaves, tough stems removed**

**1 1/2 cups (375 g) fresh ricotta cheese**

**2 teaspoons freshly grated nutmeg**

**12 dried cannelloni tubes**

**3 cups (750 g) peeled plum tomatoes, pressed through a fine-mesh strainer (passata)**

Serves: 4
Preparation: 20 minutes
Cooking: 40 minutes
Level: 1

# LINGUINE WITH BLUE CHEESE AND WALNUTS

Cook the linguine in a large pot of salted boiling water until al dente. • Drain well and return to the pan. • Heat the apple cider vinegar and walnuts in a medium saucepan. • Pour the mixture over the linguine and add the spinach and blue cheese. • Toss well and serve hot.

**1 pound (500 g) dried linguine**

**1/3 cup (80 ml) apple cider vinegar**

**1 cup (125 g) walnuts, toasted**

**10 ounces (300 g) baby spinach leaves, tough stems removed**

**1 1/4 cups (210 g) soft blue cheese (such as Roquefort or Gorgonzola), crumbled**

**Serves: 4**
**Preparation: 5 minutes**
**Cooking: 15 minutes**
**Level: 1**

# BUCATINI WITH SMOKED SALMON

Cook the bucatini in a large pot of salted boiling water until al dente. • Cook the cream with the capers in a large frying pan over low heat for 4 minutes. • Stir in the smoked salmon and dill and simmer for 2 minutes. • Remove from the heat. • Drain the bucatini and add to the pan with the sauce. • Toss well. Garnish with the dill leaves and serve hot.

**1 pound (500 g) dried bucatini or spaghetti**

**1¼ cups (310 ml) light (single) cream**

**3 tablespoons salt-cured capers, rinsed**

**8 ounces (250 g) smoked salmon, coarsely chopped**

**1 tablespoon finely chopped fresh dill leaves, plus dill leaves to garnish**

Serves: 4
Preparation: 8 minutes
Cooking: 20 minutes
Level: 1

# RAVIOLI WITH SAGE AND LEMON BUTTER

Cook the ravioli in a large pot of salted boiling water until al dente. • Sauté the sage and lemon zest in the butter in a large frying pan over medium heat for 3 minutes • Add the lemon juice and cook for 2 minutes. • Remove from the heat. • Drain the ravioli and add to the pan with the flavored butter. • Seasonwith black pepper. Toss gently and serve hot.

- **1 pound (500 g) meat or chicken-filled ravioli**
- **16 leaves fresh sage**
- **Finely grated zest and juice of 2 lemons**
- **2/3 cup (150 g) butter, cut up**
- **Freshly ground black pepper**

Serves: 4
Preparation: 5 minutes
Cooking: 10 minutes
Level: 1

■■■ *The sage and butter sauce is also good with spinach ravioli. Leave out the lemon juice, if desired.*

■ ■ ■ *Sage originally comes from Southern Europe and the Mediterranean, where it is a recurrent ingredient in many classic dishes. In northern Italian cuisine it is often mixed with melted butter to create a sublime (and quick and easy) sauce for fresh or filled pasta.* Fegato alla salvia *(liver with sage) is another classic Italian dish, from Venice. There are many different species of sage, and they are all members of the mint family. The common kind,* Salvia officinalis, *has a robust flavor that combines well with meat dishes. But there are milder kinds, such as Greek sage, that can be used to flavor milder dishes.*

# ORECCHIETTE WITH BROCCOLI AND PINE NUTS

Cook the orecchiette in a large pot of salted boiling water until al dente. • Cook the broccoli in a medium saucepan of boiling water for 5 minutes. • Drain and rinse in ice-cold water to stop the cooking process. • Mix the crème fraîche and pesto in a large frying pan and warm over low heat for 2 minutes. • Add the broccoli and pine nuts and cook for 1 minute. • Remove from the heat. • Drain the orecchiette and add to the pan with the sauce. • Toss well and serve hot.

**1 pound (500 g) dried orecchiette**
**10 ounces (300 g) broccoli florets**
**1 cup (250 ml) crème fraîche**
**3 tablespoons store-bought basil pesto**
**3/4 cup (135 g) pine nuts, toasted**

**Serves: 4**
**Preparation: 10 minutes**
**Cooking: 20 minutes**
**Level: 1**

# PAPPARDELLE WITH CHORIZO SAUSAGE

Cook the pappardelle in a large pot of salted boiling water until al dente. • Dry-fry the chorizo in a large frying pan over medium heat for 5 minutes until crispy. • Stir in the tomatoes and cook for 4 minutes until softened. • Remove from the heat. • Drain the pappardelle and add to the pan with the chorizo. • Add the parsley and toss well. • Sprinkle with the Parmesan and serve hot.

- **1 pound (500 g) dried pappardelle**
- **8 ounces (250 g) Spanish chorizo sausage, thickly sliced**
- **12 plum tomatoes, coarsely chopped**
- **2 tablespoons coarsely chopped fresh parsley**
- **1/2 cup (60 g) freshly grated Parmesan cheese**

**Serves: 4**
**Preparation: 10 minutes**
**Cooking: 20 minutes**
**Level: 1**

# PENNE WITH SMOKED CHICKEN AND PEAS

Cook the penne in a large pot of salted boiling water until al dente. • Warm the crème fraîche and chicken in a large frying pan over low heat for 4 minutes. • Add the peas and cook for 2 minutes. • Remove from the heat. • Drain the penne and add to the pan with the sauce. Season with black pepper. • Toss well and serve hot.

- **1 pound (500 g) penne**
- **1 cup (250 ml) crème fraîche**
- **10 ounces (300 g) cooked smoked chicken breast, coarsely shredded**
- **1 cup (125 g) fresh or frozen and thawed peas**
- **Freshly ground black pepper**

Serves: 4
Preparation: 10 minutes
Cooking: 20 minutes
Level: 1

# ANGEL HAIR PASTA WITH PESTO AND TOMATOES

Cook the pasta in a large pot of salted boiling water until al dente. • Cook the cherry tomatoes with the pesto in a large frying pan over medium heat for 4 minutes, until the tomatoes begin to soften. • Remove from the heat. • Drain the pasta and add to the pan with the tomatoes. • Add the goat cheese and season with black pepper. • Toss well and serve hot.

- **1 pound (500 g) dried angel hair pasta or capellini**
- **10 ounces (300 g) cherry tomatoes**
- **1/2 cup (125 ml) store-bought basil pesto**
- **3/4 cup (180 g) soft goat cheese**
- **Freshly ground black pepper**

**Serves: 4**
**Preparation: 5 minutes**
**Cooking: 10 minutes**
**Level: 1**

# ROTELLE WITH OLIVES AND ASPARAGUS

Cook the rotelle in a large pot of salted boiling water until al dente. • Cook the asparagus in boiling water for 2 minutes. • Drain and rinse in ice-cold water to stop the cooking process. Set aside. • Cook the olives and tomatoes with the oil in a large frying pan for 3 minutes until the tomatoes begin to soften. • Add the asparagus and remove from the heat. • Drain the rotelle and add to the pan with the sauce. • Toss well and serve hot.

- **1 pound (500 g) dried rotelle**
- **12 asparagus spears, woody ends removed and cut in half lengthwise**
- **1/2 cup (50 g) pitted (stoned) black olives**
- **1 pound (500 g) cherry tomatoes, cut in half**
- **1/4 cup (60 ml) extra-virgin olive oil**

**Serves: 4**
**Preparation: 10 minutes**
**Cooking: 15 minutes**
**Level: 1**

# RIGATONI WITH TOMATOES AND ANCHOVIES

Cook the rigatoni in a large pot of salted boiling water until al dente. • Combine the tomatoes, anchovies, and rosemary in a large frying pan. Simmer over low heat for 10 minutes. • Remove from the heat. • Drain the rigatoni and add to the pan with the sauce. • Toss well. Sprinkle with the Parmesan and serve hot.

- **1 pound (500 g) dried rigatoni**
- **3 cups (750 g) peeled and chopped tomatoes, with juice**
- **10 salt-cured anchovies, rinsed, boned, and finely chopped**
- **2 tablespoons finely chopped fresh rosemary**
- **1/2 cup (60 g) freshly grated Parmesan cheese**

**Serves: 4**
**Preparation: 10 minutes**
**Cooking: 20 minutes**
**Level: 1**

# LINGUINE WITH SCALLOPS AND LEMON



Cook the linguine in a large pot of salted boiling water until al dente. • Heat the basil and lemon zest in the oil in a large frying pan over low heat for 2 minutes. • Increase the heat to medium high, add the scallops, and sear them for 2 minutes on each side. • Add the lemon juice and warm through. • Remove from the heat. • Drain the linguine and add to the pan with the scallops. • Toss well and serve hot.

**1 pound (500 g) dried linguine**
**1 small bunch fresh basil, stems removed**
**Finely shredded zest and juice of 2 lemons**
**$^1/_3$ cup (90 ml) extra-virgin olive oil**
**1 pound (500 g) scallops, cleaned and patted dry**

Serves: 4
Preparation: 15 minutes
Cooking: 15 minutes
Level: 1

# DRIED FETTUCCINE WITH SHRIMP AND OREGANO

Cook the pasta in a large pot of salted boiling water until al dente. • Cook the capers and oregano in the oil in a large frying pan over low heat for 3 minutes. • Add the shrimp and cook for 4 minutes, turning them over, until they are pink and cooked through. • Remove from the heat. • Drain the pasta and add to the pan with the shrimp. • Toss well and serve hot.

**1 pound (500 g) dried fettuccine or other long ribbon pasta**
**2 tablespoons salt-cured capers, rinsed**
**5 tablespoons fresh oregano sprigs**
**1/3 cup (90 ml) extra-virgin olive oil**
**20 raw shrimps (prawns), shelled, heads removed, and deveined**

Serves: 4
Preparation: 20 minutes
Cooking: 20 minutes
Level: 1

# SQUID INK FETTUCCINE WITH SPICY SQUID

Cook the fettuccine in a large pot of salted boiling water until al dente. • Lay the squid pieces flat, skin side down, and score with a sharp knife in a crisscross pattern. • Sauté the chiles in the oil in a large frying pan for 2 minutes. • Add the squid and sauté for 2 minutes until it begins to change color and curl slightly. • Stir in the tomatoes and cook for 2 minutes. • Remove from the heat. • Drain the fettuccine and add to the pan with the sauce. • Toss well and serve hot.

- **1 pound (500 g) squid ink fettuccine**
- **1 pound (500 g) squid or cuttlefish, cleaned**
- **3 bird chiles (dried Thai chiles), seeded and finely chopped**
- **1/3 cup (90 ml) extra-virgin olive oil**
- **12 plum tomatoes, coarsely chopped**

**Serves: 4**
**Preparation: 20 minutes**
**Cooking: 15 minutes**
**Level: 1**

■ ■ ■ *Squid ink pasta is now readily available from Italian food stores and online suppliers.*

# POTATO GNOCCHI WITH WINTER SQUASH SAUCE

Preheat the oven to 350°F (180°C/gas 4). • Place the winter squash on a baking sheet and drizzle with the oil. • Bake for about 15 minutes, or until softened. • Transfer the winter squash to a food processor and process until smooth, gradually pouring in the cream. • Spoon the winter squash sauce into a large frying pan and set aside. • Cook the gnocchi in a large pot of salted boiling water until they rise to the surface. • Use a slotted spoon to transfer the gnocchi to the pan with the sauce. • Warm the gnocchi with the winter squash sauce until heated through. • Season with salt and serve hot.

**1¼ pounds (550 g) winter squash or pumpkin, peeled, seeded, and diced**

**¼ cup (60 ml) tarragon-infused olive oil**

**¾ cup (180 ml) heavy (double) cream**

**1 pound (500 g) potato gnocchi**

**Salt**

Serves: 4
Preparation: 20 minutes
Cooking: 25 minutes
Level: 1

■ ■ ■ *Flavored and infused oils can be purchased from many supermarkets and specialty food stores.*

# FARFALLE WITH ARTICHOKES AND ROASTED PEPPERS

Broil (grill) the bell peppers until the skins are blackened all over. • Wrap them in a paper bag for 5 minutes, then remove the skins and seeds. Slice into strips. • Cook the farfalle in a large pot of salted boiling water until al dente. • Combine the bell peppers, artichokes, and olives in a large frying pan and heat until warmed through. • Drain the farfalle and add to the pan with the sauce. Add the spinach. • Toss well and serve hot.

**2 red bell peppers (capsicums)**

**1 pound (500 g) dried farfalle**

**5 ounces (150 g) marinated artichoke hearts, cut into quarters**

**1/2 cup (50 g) pitted (stoned) black olives**

**8 ounces (250 g) baby spinach leaves, tough stems removed**

Serves: 4
Preparation: 20 minutes + 5 minutes to rest
Cooking: 20 minutes
Level: 1

# PAPPARDELLE WITH PANCETTA AND ARUGULA

Cook the pappardelle in a large pot of salted boiling water until al dente. • Dry-fry the pancetta in a large frying pan over medium heat for 3 minutes, until crispy. • Add the tomatoes and cook for 3 minutes. • Drain the pappardelle and add to the pan with the pancetta and tomatoes. • Add the arugula and Parmesan. • Toss well and serve hot.

**1 pound (500 g) dried pappardelle**
**20 slices pancetta or bacon**
**1 pound (500 g) cherry tomatoes, cut in half**
**2 cups (100 g) arugula (rocket) leaves**
**1/2 cup (60 g) shaved Parmesan cheese**

Serves: 4
Preparation: 5 minutes
Cooking: 20 minutes
Level: 1

# PENNE WITH SWEET POTATOES AND FETA

Preheat the oven to 400°F (200°C/ gas 6). • Place the sweet potatoes on a baking sheet and drizzle with 2 tablespoons of the oil. • Bake for about 15 minutes, or until softened. • Cook the penne in a large pot of salted boiling water until al dente. • Drain well and return to the pan. • Sauté the leeks in the remaining 2 tablespoons of oil in a large frying pan over medium heat for 3 minutes. • Stir in the penne, sweet potatoes, and feta. • Toss well and serve hot.

- **2 sweet potatoes, peeled and diced**
- **1/4 cup (60 ml) rosemary-infused olive oil**
- **1 pound (500 g) dried penne**
- **2 leeks, thinly shredded**
- **6 ounces (180 g) marinated feta cheese**

**Serves: 4**
**Preparation: 10 minutes**
**Cooking: 25 minutes**
**Level: 1**

# PENNE WITH CREAMY BACON SAUCE

Cook the penne in a large pot of salted boiling water until al dente. • Dry-fry the bacon in a large frying pan over medium heat for 3 minutes, until crispy. • Add the cream, garlic, and Parmesan and cook over low heat for 4 minutes. • Drain the penne and add to the pan with the sauce. • Toss well and serve hot.

**1 pound (500 g) dried penne**

**8 slices bacon, thinly sliced**

**1¼ cups (310 ml) heavy (double) cream**

**3 cloves garlic, finely chopped**

**½ cup (60 g) freshly grated Parmesan cheese**

Serves: 4
Preparation: 5 minutes
Cooking: 20 minutes
Level: 1

# SPAGHETTI MARINARA

Cook the spaghetti in a large pot of salted boiling water until al dente. • Combine the tomatoes, olives, and garlic in a medium saucepan over low heat and cook for 5 minutes. • Add the seafood and cook over low heat for about 5 minutes, or until the seafood is cooked. • Drain the spaghetti and add to the pan with the seafood sauce. • Toss well and serve hot.

**1 pound (500 g) dried spaghetti**

**3 cups (750 g) peeled and chopped tomatoes, with juice**

**1/2 cup (50 g) pitted (stoned) black olives, coarsely chopped**

**3 cloves garlic, finely chopped**

**12 ounces (350 g) mixed seafood (mussels, clams etc.)**

**Serves: 4**
**Preparation: 5 minutes**
**Cooking: 20 minutes**
**Level: 1**

■ ■ ■ *You can use fresh or frozen mixed seafood for this recipe. If using frozen seafood, make sure that you thaw the mixture before cooking.*

# ANGEL HAIR PASTA WITH ANCHOVIES AND GARLIC

Cook the pasta in a large pot of salted boiling water until al dente. • Heat the oil in a large frying pan over medium heat. Add the anchovies and let them dissolve for about 5 minutes, taking care not to let them burn. • Add the garlic and parsley and cook for 1 minute. • Drain the pasta and add to the pan with the anchovies. • Toss well and serve hot.

**1 pound (500 g) dried angel hair pasta or capellini**

**1/3 cup (90 ml) extra-virgin olive oil**

**8 salt-cured anchovies, rinsed, boned, and finely chopped**

**8 cloves garlic, finely chopped**

**4 tablespoons finely chopped fresh parsley**

Serves: 4
Preparation: 5 minutes
Cooking: 15 minutes
Level: 1

331

# PASTA WITH CREAMY SUN-DRIED TOMATO SAUCE

Cook the pasta in a large pot of salted boiling water until al dente. • Combine the sun-dried tomatoes, onion, and cream in a large frying pan and cook over low heat for 5 minutes. • Add the Parmesan and cook for 2 minutes. • Drain the pasta and add to the pan with the sauce. • Toss well and serve hot.

- **1 pound (500 g) large elbow macaroni (pipe rigate)**
- **12 sun-dried tomatoes, finely chopped**
- **1 large onion, finely chopped**
- **1¹/4 cups (310 ml) light (single) cream**
- **¹/2 cup (60 g) freshly grated Parmesan cheese**

**Serves: 4**
**Preparation: 8 minutes**
**Cooking: 20 minutes**
**Level: 1**

# FETTUCCINE ALFREDO



Cook the fettuccine in a large pot of salted boiling water until al dente. • Melt the butter in a large frying pan. • Add the cream and Parmesan and cook over low heat for 4 minutes. • Stir in the parsley. • Drain the fettuccine and add to the pan with the sauce. • Toss well and serve hot.

**1 pound (500 g) dried fettuccine**

**1/3 cup (90 g) butter, cut up**

**1 1/4 cups (310 ml) light (single) cream**

**1/2 cup (60 g) freshly grated Parmesan cheese**

**3 tablespoons finely chopped fresh parsley**

Serves: 4
Preparation: 5 minutes
Cooking: 15 minutes
Level: 1

# LINGUINE CARBONARA

Cook the linguine in a large pot of salted boiling water until al dente. • Dry-fry the bacon in a large frying pan over medium heat for 3 minutes, until crispy. Set aside. • Beat the eggs with the cream and Parmesan in a medium bowl. • Add the bacon. • Drain the linguine and return to the pan. Pour in the egg mixture and cook over very low heat for 2 minutes, until the sauce begins to thicken and the eggs are cooked through. • Toss well and serve hot.

- **1 pound (500 g) dried linguine**
- **8 slices bacon, thinly sliced**
- **4 large eggs**
- **$1^1/4$ cups (310 ml) light (single) cream**
- **$^1/2$ cup (60 g) freshly grated Parmesan cheese**

**Serves: 4**
**Preparation: 10 minutes**
**Cooking: 15 minutes**
**Level: 1**

■ ■ ■ *Carbonara is a classic pasta sauce in modern Roman cuisine. It first appeared at the end of World War II, and many believe that it was invented in the Eternal City when Allied troops arrived and began dispensing their military rations—of which bacon and eggs were key elements.*

# FETTUCCINE WITH CHICKEN AND OLIVE TAPENADE

Cook the pasta in a large pot of salted boiling water until al dente. • Fry the chicken in the oil in a large frying pan over medium heat for 5 minutes, or until cooked through. • Drain the pasta and return to the pan. Stir in the chicken, olive tapenade, and arugula. • Toss well and serve hot.

**1 pound (500 g) dried fettuccine**

**2 boneless, skinless chicken breast halves, cut into thin strips**

**3 tablespoons extra-virgin olive oil**

**3 tablespoons olive tapenade**

**2 cups (100 g) arugula (rocket) leaves**

Serves: 4
Preparation: 5 minutes
Cooking: 15 minutes
Level: 1

# ORECCHIETTE WITH ROASTED BELL PEPPERS

Broil (grill) the bell peppers until the skins are blackened all over. • Wrap them in a paper bag for 5 minutes, then remove the skins and seeds. Slice into strips. • Cook the orecchiette in a large pot of salted boiling water until al dente. • Transfer the bell peppers to a food processor. Process until smooth, gradually pouring in the cream. • Pour the bell pepper sauce into a large frying pan and cook over low heat for 3 minutes. • Drain the orecchiette and add to the pan with the sauce. • Stir in the spinach and feta. • Toss well and serve hot.

- **4 red bell peppers (capsicums)**
- **1 pound (500 g) dried orecchiette**
- **1 cup (250 ml) light (single) cream**
- **2 cups (100 g) baby spinach leaves, tough stems removed**
- **6 ounces (180 g) feta cheese, cut into cubes**

**Serves: 4**
**Preparation: 20 minutes**
**Cooking: 25 minutes**
**Level: 1**

# FARFALLE WITH FENNEL AND STUFFED OLIVES

Cook the farfalle in a large pot of salted boiling water until al dente. • Cook the fennel and lemon zest in the oil in a large frying pan over low heat for 4 minutes. • Add the olives and lemon juice. Cook for 3 minutes. • Drain the farfalle and add to the pan with the fennel. • Toss well and serve hot.

**1 pound (500 g) dried farfalle**

**2 baby fennel, thinly sliced**

**Finely grated zest and juice of 2 lemons**

**1/4 cup (60 ml) extra-virgin olive oil**

**1/2 cup (50 g) green olives stuffed with anchovies, cut in half**

**Serves: 4**
**Preparation: 10 minutes**
**Cooking: 15 minutes**
**Level: 1**

# CREAMY CHICKEN AND MUSHROOM FETTUCCINE

Cook the fettuccine in a large pot of salted boiling water until al dente. • Cook the chicken, mushrooms, and 3/4 cup (180 ml) of the cream in a large frying pan over medium heat for 5 minutes, until the chicken is cooked through. • Add the remaining 1/2 cup (125 ml) cream and Parmesan and simmer over low heat for 2 minutes. • Drain the fettuccine and add to the pan with the sauce. • Serve hot.

- **1 pound (500 g) dried fettuccine**
- **2 boneless, skinless chicken breasts**
- **12 ounces (350 g) mushrooms, thinly sliced**
- **1 1/4 cups (300 ml) heavy (double) cream**
- **1/2 cup (60 g) freshly grated Parmesan cheese**

**Serves: 4**
**Preparation: 10 minutes**
**Cooking: 15 minutes**
**Level: 1**

# NOODLES

# SOBA NOODLES WITH SNOW PEAS AND BABY CORN

Cook the noodles in plenty of boiling water for 5–7 minutes, or until tender. • If using fresh baby corn, blanch it in boiling water for 2 minutes. • Add the snow peas and boil for 1 minute. • Drain and rinse under ice-cold water to stop the cooking process. • Drain the noodles and transfer to a large bowl. • Mix in the sesame oil and lemon juice. • Add the baby corn and snow peas. • Toss well and serve hot.

- **1 1/4 pounds (600 g) dried buckwheat noodles**
- **12 fresh or canned baby corn, sliced in half lengthwise**
- **24 snow peas (sugar peas/mangetout), trimmed**
- **3 tablespoons Asian sesame oil**
- **3 tablespoons freshly squeezed lemon juice**

Serves: 4–6
Preparation: 5 minutes
Cooking: 10 minutes
Level: 1

■ ■ ■ *Soba noodles are a Japanese specialty made from buckwheat flour. They have a refined yet earthy taste and are served both hot and at room temperature. You can find them wherever Japanese foods are sold*

# SOBA NOODLES WITH BLACK SESAME

Cook the soba noodles in plenty of boiling water for 5–7 minutes, or until tender. • Drain and rinse under cold running water. • Place the noodles in a large bowl and set aside. • Mix the rice wine vinegar and soy sauce in a small bowl. • Pour the mixture over the noodles. • Add the cilantro and sesame seeds. • Toss well and serve at room temperature.

**1¼ pounds (600 g) dried soba noodles (see note, page 348)**
**⅓ cup (90 ml) rice wine vinegar**
**⅓ cup (90 ml) soy sauce**
**1 cup (50 g) fresh cilantro (coriander) leaves**
**3 tablespoons black sesame seeds**

**Serves: 4–6**
**Preparation: 5 minutes**
**Cooking: 7 minutes**
**Level: 1**

■ ■ ■ *Black sesame seeds are prized for their earthy flavor. Replace with ivory-colored sesame seeds if that's what you have on hand. Both types are rich in protein and nutrients.*

# SATAY BEEF WITH RICE NOODLES

Put the noodles in a medium bowl, cover with boiling water, and soak until softened, 5–10 minutes. • Drain and set aside. • Place a wok over high heat. • When it is very hot, add the sesame oil. • Add the beef and stir-fry for 2 minutes. • Add the bell peppers and stir-fry for 2 minutes. • Stir in the satay sauce and heat for 1 minute. • Add the noodles. • Toss well and serve hot.

**14 ounces (400 g) dried rice stick noodles**

**3 tablespoons sesame oil**

**1¼ pounds (600 g) tenderloin beef, cut into thin strips**

**2 red bell peppers (capsicums), seeded and cut into thin strips**

**¾ cup (180 ml) store-bought satay sauce**

**Serves: 4**
**Preparation: 10 minutes + 5–10 minutes to soak noodles**
**Cooking: 5 minutes**
**Level: 1**

■ ■ ■ *Thin rice stick noodles are white and about the length of a chopstick. Instead of cooking them, soak in boiling water until softened, usually 5–10 minutes. Refer to the package for exact soaking times. Satay sauce is available in many supermarkets or wherever Asian foods are sold.*

# RICE NOODLES WITH SHRIMP AND CILANTRO

Put the noodles in a medium bowl, cover with boiling water, and soak until softened, 5–10 minutes. • Drain and set aside. • Place a wok over high heat. • When it is very hot, add the sesame oil. • Add the shrimp and cook for 4 minutes, turning often, until pink and cooked through. • Add the lime juice and noodles and toss well. • Remove from the heat and stir in the cilantro. • Serve hot.

**14 ounces (400 g) dried rice vermicelli noodles**

**1/3 cup (90 ml) Asian sesame oil**

**20 raw large shrimp (prawn), peeled and deveined**

**1/3 cup (90 ml) freshly squeezed lime juice**

**3/4 cup (40 g) fresh cilantro (coriander) leaves**

Serves: 4
Preparation: 10 minutes + 5–10 minutes to soak noodles
Cooking: 5 minutes
Level: 1

# GRILLED HOISIN CHICKEN WITH SNOW PEAS

Combine the chicken and 1/2 cup (125 ml) of the hoisin sauce in a medium bowl. Let marinate for 1 hour. • Place the noodles in a medium bowl, cover with boiling water, and soak until softened, 5–10 minutes. • Drain and set aside. • Cook the snow peas in boiling water for 1 minute. • Drain and rinse under ice-cold water to stop the cooking process. • Place a grill pan over medium-high heat. • Grill the chicken on each side for 3–4 minutes, or until cooked through. • Slice the chicken thinly and set aside. • Mix the noodles, snow peas, peanuts, and remaining 1/4 cup (60 ml) hoisin sauce in a large bowl. • Top with the chicken and serve hot.

- **1 pound (500 g) skinless, boneless chicken breasts, sliced**
- **3/4 cup (180 ml) hoisin sauce**
- **14 ounces (400 g) dried vermicelli rice noodles**
- **8 ounces (250 g) snow peas (mangetout), trimmed**
- **1/2 cup (80 g) salted roasted peanuts**

Serves: 4
Preparation: 15 minutes + 1 hour to marinate
Cooking: 4–5 minutes
Level: 1

# NOODLES WITH BEEF AND BLACK BEAN SAUCE

Place the noodles in a medium bowl, cover with boiling water, and soak until softened, 5–10 minutes. • Drain and set aside. • Place a wok over high heat. • When it is very hot, add the sesame oil. • Add the beef and stir-fry for 2 minutes. • Add the bell peppers and stir-fry for 2 minutes. • Stir in the black bean sauce and heat for 1 minute. • Add the noodles. • Toss well and serve hot.

**14 ounces (400 g) dried rice stick noodles**

**3 tablespoons Asian sesame oil**

**1¼ pounds (600 g) tenderloin beef, cut into thin strips**

**2 green bell peppers (capsicums), seeded and diced**

**¾ cup (180 ml) Chinese black bean sauce**

Serves: 4
Preparation: 10 minutes + 5–10 minutes to soak noodles
Cooking: 5 minutes
Level: 1

# CHICKEN LAKSA NOODLES

Cook the hokkien noodles in plenty of boiling water until tender. Refer to the package for exact cooking time. • Drain and set aside. • Place a wok over high heat. • Cook the laksa paste for 30 seconds until aromatic. • Pour in the coconut milk and chicken stock and bring to a boil. • Decrease the heat to low and add the chicken. Cook for 6 minutes. • Add the noodles and cook for 2 minutes. • Serve hot.

**14 ounces (400 g) fresh hokkien or Shanghai noodles**

**1 cup (250 ml) laksa paste**

**1 2/3 cups (400 ml) coconut milk**

**1 1/2 cups (375 ml) chicken stock**

**8 ounces (250 g) skinless, boneless chicken breast, thinly sliced**

**Serves:** 4
**Preparation:** 5 minutes
**Cooking:** 15 minutes
**Level:** 1

■ ■ ■ *Hokkien noodles are sold fresh, in refrigerated packages. If unavailable, substitute 12 ounces (350 g) dried spaghetti and cook according to the package instructions. Laksa is an Indonesian and Malaysian noodle dish made with chicken in a creamy curry sauce. Laksa paste is available in some Asian food stores and online.*

# GINGER NOODLES WITH VEGETABLE RIBBONS

Cook the noodles in plenty of boiling water until tender, 3–5 minutes. Refer to the package for exact cooking time. • Drain and set aside. • Place a wok over high heat. • When it is very hot, add the carrots, zucchini, oyster sauce, and ginger. Cook for 2 minutes. • Add the noodles and cook for 2 minutes. • Toss well and serve hot.

**1¼ pounds (600 g) fresh Chinese egg noodles (or tagliatelle)**

**2 medium carrots, cut lengthwise into thin ribbons**

**2 medium zucchini (courgettes), cut lengthwise into thin ribbons**

**½ cup (125 ml) oyster sauce**

**1 tablespoon freshly grated ginger**

**Serves:** 4–6
**Preparation:** 10 minutes
**Cooking:** 10 minutes
**Level:** 1

■ ■ ■ *Chinese egg noodles are very similar to Italian tagliatelle. Substitute with fresh tagliatelle.*

# SMOKED SALMON NOODLE SALAD

Place the noodles in a medium bowl, cover with boiling water, and soak until softened, 5–10 minutes. • Drain and transfer to a large bowl. • Cook the sugar snap peas in boiling water for 1 minute. • Drain and rinse under ice-cold water to stop the cooking process. • Mix the sugar snap peas and smoked salmon into the noodles. • Add the sweet chili sauce and lime juice. • Toss well and serve at room temperature.

**1¼ pounds (600 g) dried rice stick noodles**

**8 ounces (250 g) sugar snap peas, trimmed**

**4 ounces (125 g) smoked salmon, sliced and coarsely chopped**

**⅓ cup (90 ml) Thai sweet chili sauce**

**2 tablespoons freshly squeezed lime juice**

**Serves: 4–6**
**Preparation: 5 minutes + 5–10 minutes to soak noodles**
**Cooking: 5 minutes**
**Level: 1**

# SOBA NOODLE WITH SEAWEED



Cook the soba noodles in plenty of boiling water for 5–7 minutes, or until tender. • Drain and transfer to a large bowl. • Cook the arame in boiling water for 7 minutes. • Drain well and add to the noodles. • Mix in the pickled ginger, cucumbers, and sweet chile sauce. • Toss well and serve at room temperature.

**14 ounces (400 g) dried soba noodles (see note, page 348)**

**2 ounces (60 g) arame seaweed, rinsed**

**1/2 cup (150 g) firmly packed sliced pickled ginger**

**2 cucumbers, with peel, cut lengthwise into thin strips**

**1/2 cup (125 ml) Thai sweet chili sauce**

**Serves: 4**
**Preparation: 5 minutes**
**Cooking: 12–15 minutes**
**Level: 1**

■ ■ ■ *Arame seaweed is dried and then shredded. It has a mild flavor and is used to flavor many Japanese dishes. Pickled ginger, usually preserved in rice wine, is deliciously sweet and slightly spicy.*

# PORK LO MEIN

Cook the noodles in plenty of boiling water until tender, 3–5 minutes. Refer to the package for exact cooking time. • Drain and set aside. • Place a wok over high heat. • When it is very hot, add the pork and five-spice powder. Cook for 3 minutes. • Add the soy sauce and cabbage. Cook for 2 minutes. • Add the noodles and cook for 2 minutes. • Toss well and serve hot.

**1½ pounds (600 g) fresh thin Chinese egg noodles (or tagliolini)**

**1 pound (500 g) ground (minced) pork**

**1 tablespoon five-spice powder**

**⅓ cup (90 ml) soy sauce**

**½ Chinese cabbage (wombok), finely shredded**

Serves: 4–6
Preparation: 5 minutes
Cooking: 10 minutes
Level: 1

# PORK AND ASPARAGUS STIR-FRY

Cook the noodles in plenty of boiling water until tender. Refer to the package for exact cooking time. • Drain and set aside. • Cook the asparagus in boiling water for 3 minutes. • Drain and rinse under ice-cold water to stop the cooking process. • Place a wok over high heat. • When it is very hot, add the sesame oil. • Stir-fry the pork for 3 minutes. • Add the asparagus and stir-fry for 2 minutes. • Add the oyster sauce and noodles and cook for 2 minutes. • Toss well and serve hot.

- **1¼ pounds (600 g) hokkien or Shanghai noodles (or substitute 1 pound /500 g dried spaghetti)**
- **8 ounces (250 g) asparagus, woody ends removed and cut in half**
- **3 tablespoons Asian sesame oil**
- **12 ounces (350 g) pork tenderloin, cut into small pieces**
- **¾ cup (180 ml) oyster sauce**

**Serves: 4–6**
**Preparation: 10 minutes**
**Cooking: 15 minutes**
**Level: 1**

# COCONUT SHRIMP NOODLES

Place the noodles in a medium bowl, cover with boiling water, and soak until softened, 5–10 minutes. • Drain and transfer to a large bowl. • Mix the cream of coconut and fish sauce in a medium saucepan. • Add the shrimp and cook over medium heat for 4 minutes, until they are pink and cooked through. • Remove from the heat and add to the noodles. • Add the mint. • Toss well and serve hot.

**14 ounces (400 g) dried vermicelli rice noodles**

**1 cup (250 ml) cream of coconut**

**1 tablespoon Vietnamese or Thai fish sauce**

**14 ounces (400 g) raw shrimp (prawn), peeled and deveined**

**3 tablespoons leaves fresh mint**

Serves: 4
Preparation: 10 minutes + 5–10 minutes to soak noodles
Cooking: 5 minutes
Level: 1

# PEKING DUCK AND UDON NOODLE SOUP

Remove the flesh from the duck and coarsely shred it. • Combine the stock and star anise in a large saucepan and bring to a boil. • Add the udon noodles and cook for 4 minutes. • Add the duck and cook for 3 minutes. • Stir in the snow pea shoots. • Serve hot.

**1 store-bought cooked Peking duck**

**5 cups (1 liter) chicken stock**

**1 star anise**

**14 ounces (400 g) udon noodles**

**8 ounces (250 g) snow pea shoots**

Serves: 4
Preparation: 10 minutes
Cooking: 10 minutes
Level: 1

■ ■ ■ *Udon noodles are Japanese noodles made from wheat flour. They are usually served in broth or stock. Peking ducks are available wherever there are Chinese markets and large ethnic populations. Snow pea shoots are available in natural food stores and Chinese markets.*

# STIR-FRIED CHICKEN NOODLES WITH PLUM SAUCE

Cook the noodles in plenty of boiling water until softened, about 5–10 minutes. • Drain and set aside. • Cook the snake beans in boiling water for 2 minutes. • Drain and rinse under ice-cold water to stop the cooking process. • Place a wok over high heat. • When it is very hot, add the sesame oil. • Add the chicken and stir-fry for 4 minutes. • Stir in the plum sauce and beans. Cook for 2 minutes. • Add the noodles and cook for 2 minutes. • Toss well and serve hot.

**14 ounces (400 g) Chinese or Italian dried wheat noodles**

**2 cups (200 g) snake beans, trimmed and cut into short lengths**

**3 tablespoons Asian sesame oil**

**12 ounces (350 g) chicken breast, thinly sliced**

**3/4 cup (180 ml) store-bought Chinese plum sauce**

Serves: 4
Preparation: 10 minutes
Cooking: 15–20 minutes
Level: 1

■ ■ ■ *Snake beans go by a host of different names, including asparagus beans, pea beans, cowpeas, catjang, yard-long beans, and China peas. They have a refreshing delicate flavor. Substitute green beans if you can't find them.*

# BELL PEPPER AND NOODLE STIR-FRY

Cook the noodles in plenty of boiling water until softened, about 5–10 minutes. • Drain and set aside. • Place a wok over high heat. • When it is very hot, add the sesame oil. • Add the bell peppers and eggplants. Stir-fry for 3 minutes. • Add the oyster sauce and noodles. Cook for 2 minutes. • Toss well and serve hot.

- **14 ounces (400 g) dried Chinese egg noodles (or tagliatelle)**
- **3 tablespoons Asian sesame oil**
- **2 red bell peppers (capsicums), seeded and cut into thin strips**
- **4 baby eggplants (aubergines), thinly sliced**
- **3/4 cup (180 ml) oyster sauce**

**Serves: 4**
**Preparation: 10 minutes**
**Cooking: 10–15 minutes**
**Level: 1**

■ ■ ■ *Bell peppers, also known simply as peppers or capsicums, are native to South America but they have been adopted by cuisines around the world. Available in four main colors—red, green, orange, and yellow—their tasty flesh makes a welcome addition to salads and stir-fries. Bell peppers are rich in vitamins A and C and in carotenoids.*



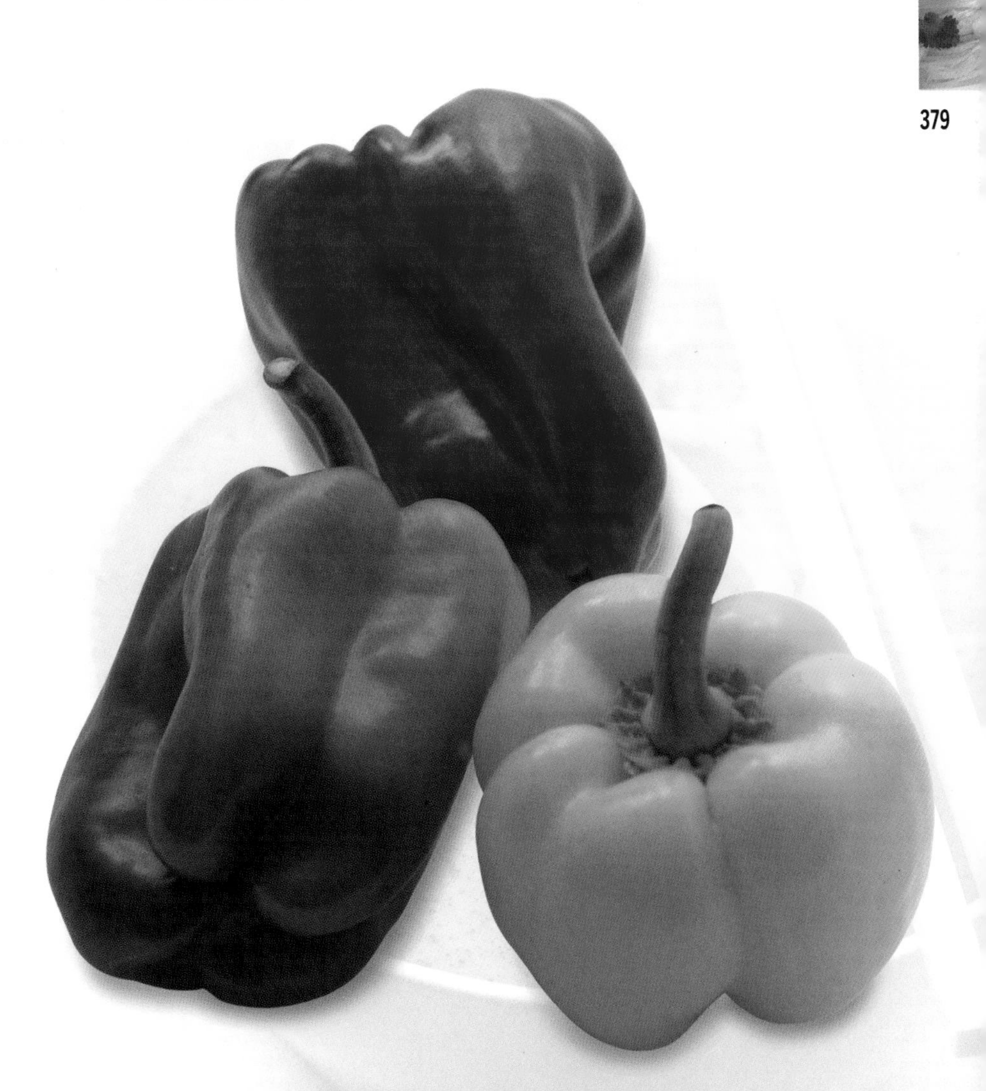

# NOODLES WITH SQUID, TOMATO, AND BASIL

Place the noodles in a medium bowl, cover with boiling water and soak until softened, 5–10 minutes. • Drain and set aside. • Cut the squid into bite-size pieces. Lay the squid pieces flat, skin side down, and score with a sharp knife in a crisscross pattern. • Place a wok over high heat. • When it is very hot, add the sesame oil. • Add the squid and stir-fry for 2 minutes, until it begins to change color and curl slightly. • Add the cherry tomatoes and cook for 1 minute. • Add the noodles and basil. • Toss well and serve hot.

**1¼ pounds (600 g) dried thick rice noodles**

**12 ounces (350 g) squid, cleaned**

**3 tablespoons Asian sesame oil**

**12 ounces (350 g) cherry tomatoes, cut into quarters**

**4 tablespoons fresh basil leaves**

Serves: 6
Preparation: 10 minutes + 5 minutes to soak noodles
Cooking: 3 minutes
Level: 1

# EGG NOODLE STIR-FRY



Place the noodles in a medium bowl, cover with boiling water and soak for 3 minutes. • Drain and set aside. • Heat a wok over high heat. • When it is very hot, add the sesame oil. • Pour in the beaten eggs. • When the bottoms are set, slide a wooden spatula under the eggs to loosen them from the pan. Shake the pan with a rotating movement to spread. • Cook until nicely browned on the underside and set on top. • Remove from the heat and slice into strips. Set aside. • Add the pea and corn mix to the wok and cook for 30 seconds. • Add the soy sauce, egg strips, and noodles. Cook for 2 minutes. • Toss well and serve hot.

**14 ounces (400 g) instant noodles**

**3 tablespoons Asian sesame oil**

**8 large eggs, lightly beaten**

**1 cup (150 g) frozen pea and corn mix, thawed**

**$^{1}/_{3}$ cup (90 ml) soy sauce**

**Serves: 4**
**Preparation: 5 minutes + 3 minutes to soak noodles**
**Cooking: 5 minutes**
**Level: 1**

■ ■ ■ *If you can't find instant noodles, substitute ramen noodles, discarding the flavor packet.*

# CHICKEN AND CASHEW NOODLES

Combine the chicken and 1/2 cup (125 ml) oyster sauce in a medium bowl. Let marinate for 1 hour. • Cook the noodles in plenty of boiling water until softened, about 5 minutes. • Drain and set aside. • Place a wok over high heat. • Add the chicken and marinade and cook for 4 minutes until browned. • Add the noodles and remaining 1/4 cup (60 ml) oyster sauce. Cook for 2 minutes. • Add the spinach and cashew nuts. • Toss well and serve hot.

**12 ounces (350 g) skinless, boneless chicken breasts, diced**

**3/4 cup (180 ml) oyster sauce**

**14 ounces (400 g) dried thin Chinese egg noodles (or thin spaghetti)**

**2 cups (100 g) baby spinach leaves**

**3/4 cup (120 g) cashew nuts, toasted**

Serves: 4
Preparation: 10 minutes + 1 hour to marinate
Cooking: 15 minutes
Level: 1

# THAI GREEN FISH CURRY

Cook the hokkien noodles in plenty of boiling water until tender. Refer to the package for exact cooking time. • Drain and set aside. • Place a wok over high heat. • Cook the curry paste for 30 seconds until aromatic. • Pour in the coconut milk and lime juice and bring to a boil. • Decrease the heat to low. Add the fish and cook for 3 minutes. • Add the noodles and cook for 2 minutes. • Serve hot.

**14 ounces (400 g) fresh hokkien or Shanghai noodles (see page 360)**

**2 tablespoons Thai green curry paste (see page 138)**

**1¾ cups (400 ml) coconut milk**

**1 tablespoon freshly squeezed lime juice**

**12 ounces (350 g) firm-textured white fish (such as cod or haddock), cut into small pieces**

Serves: 4
Preparation: 5 minutes
Cooking: 15 minutes
Level: 1

# CHICKEN TOM YUM NOODLES

Cook the hokkien noodles in plenty of boiling water until tender. Refer to the package for exact cooking time. • Drain and set aside. • Place a wok over high heat. • Cook the tom yum paste for 30 seconds until aromatic. • Add the chicken stock and lime juice and bring to a boil. • Decrease the heat to low and add the chicken. Cook for 4 minutes until browned. • Add the noodles and cook for 2 minutes. • Serve hot.

**$1^1/4$ pounds (600 g) fresh hokkien or Shanghai noodles (or substitute 1 pound/500 g dried spaghetti)**

**$2^1/2$ tablespoons tom yum paste**

**3 cups (750 ml) chicken stock**

**1 tablespoon freshly squeezed lime juice**

**12 ounces (350 g) boneless, skinless chicken breast, thinly sliced**

**Serves: 6**
**Preparation: 5 minutes**
**Cooking: 15 minutes**
**Level: 1**

■ ■ ■ *Tom yum paste is made by crushing and stir-frying lemongrass, kaffir lime leaves, galangal, shallots, lime juice, fish sauce, tamarind, and chilies. It can be purchased from ethnic food stores and online Thai food suppliers.*

# HOISIN CHICKEN NOODLE STIR-FRY

Coat the chicken with 1/2 cup (125 ml) the hoisin sauce in a large bowl. Cover with plastic wrap (cling film) and refrigerate for 1 hour. • Cook the noodles in a large pot of salted boiling water for about 5 minutes, or until al dente. • Drain and set aside. • Cook the broccoli in boiling water for 2 minutes. • Drain and set aside. • Place a wok over high heat. • When it is very hot, add the chicken and the remaining 1/2 cup (125 ml) of hoisin sauce. Cook for 2 minutes. • Add the bell peppers and broccoli and cook for 2 minutes. • Add the noodles and cook for 1 minute. • Serve hot.

**2** **boneless, skinless chicken breasts, cut into small pieces**

**1** **cup (250 ml) hoisin sauce**

**14** **ounces (400 g) fresh hokkien or Shanghai noodles** **(see page 360)**

**1** **bunch kai-lan or Chinese broccoli, cut into short lengths**

**2** **red bell peppers (capsicums), seeded and cut into thin strips**

**Serves: 4**
**Preparation: 10 minutes + 1 hour to marinate**
**Cooking: 12 minutes**
**Level: 1**

# SOY CHICKEN NOODLES

Coat the chicken with the soy sauce in a medium bowl. Cover with plastic wrap (cling film) and refrigerate for 1 hour. • Place a grill pan over medium-high heat. • Grill the chicken for 5 minutes on each side until cooked through. • Let rest in a warm place for 5 minutes. • Cover the noodles with boiling water in a medium bowl and soak for 5 minutes. • Drain and set aside. • Shred the chicken and put in a large bowl. Add the noodles, cucumber, and mint. • Toss well and serve at room temperature.

**2 boneless, skinless chicken breasts**

**1/4 cup (60 ml) soy sauce**

**14 ounces (400 g) dried rice vermicelli noodles**

**1 cucumber, shaved lengthwise into ribbons**

**2 tablespoons leaves fresh mint**

Serves: 4
Preparation: 10 minutes + 1 hour to marinate
Cooking: 10 minutes
Level: 1

# RICE NOODLES WITH MUSHROOMS AND EGG

Cover the noodles with boiling water in a medium bowl and soak for 5 minutes. • Drain and set aside. • Beat the eggs and 2 tablespoons of the soy sauce in a large bowl. • Heat 1 tablespoon of the oil in a large frying pan. • Pour in the egg mixture. When the bottom has set, slide a wooden spatula under the eggs to loosen them from the pan. Shake the pan with a rotating movement to spread the eggs and cook until nicely browned on the underside and the top is set. • Remove from the heat and slice into strips. Set aside. • Sauté the mushrooms in the remaining 2 tablespoons of oil in a large frying pan over medium heat for 3 minutes. • Add the noodles, the remaining soy sauce, and egg strips. • Toss well and serve hot.

- **8 ounces (250 g) dried thick rice noodles**
- **6 large eggs**
- **1/3 cup (90 ml) soy sauce**
- **3 tablespoons Asian sesame oil**
- **1 pound (500 g) shiitake mushrooms, stems discarded and caps thinly sliced**

**Serves: 4**
**Preparation: 15 minutes**
**Cooking: 10 minutes**
**Level: 1**

# SEAFOOD

# STEAMED MUSSELS WITH TOMATOES AND BASIL

Heat the oil in a large saucepan over medium heat. • Add the tomatoes and cook for 3 minutes. • Pour in the wine and cook for 2 more minutes. • Increase the heat to high and add the mussels. • Cook for 7–10 minutes, or until the mussels open. Discard any that have not opened. • Add the basil and toss to combine well. • Serve hot.

**3 tablespoons (45 ml) extra-virgin olive oil**

**8 large tomatoes, diced**

**1 cup (250 ml) dry white wine**

**2 pounds (1 kg) mussels, in shells, cleaned and beards removed**

**4 tablespoons finely chopped fresh basil + extra whole leaves to garnish**

Serves: 4
Preparation: 15 minutes + time to clean mussels
Cooking: 10 minutes
Level: 1

■ ■ ■ *To clean mussels: Wash in several changes of cold water. Wash carefully, discarding any with broken shells, and pulling off any "beard" (weedy growth) clinging to the shells. If you have the time, place the mussels in a pot under slowly running cold water for 1 hour.*

# STUFFED MUSSELS

Preheat the oven to 400°F (200°C/gas 6). • Combine the bread crumbs, cheese, parsley, anchovies, and reserved oil in a medium bowl. • Open the mussels by inserting a short strong knife or oyster shucker near the hinge and twist to open the shell. Discard the top shells. • Place the mussels on a baking sheet and cover each one with about 1 tablespoon of the bread crumb mixture. • Bake for 10–12 minutes. • Serve hot.

**1½ cups (100 g) fresh bread crumbs**
**¼ cup (50 g) freshly grated Parmesan cheese**
**1 cup (50 g) finely chopped fresh parsley**
**4 anchovy fillets, preserved in oil, ¼ cup (60 ml) of the oil reserved**
**24 mussels, in shells, cleaned and beards removed**

Serves: 2
Preparation: 20 minutes + time to clean mussels
Cooking: 10–12 minutes
Level: 1

# MUSSELS WITH SAFFRON SAUCE

Combine the wine and saffron in a large saucepan over medium-low heat and bring to a gentle simmer. • Add the tomatoes and simmer for 3 minutes. • Increase the heat to medium and add the mussels.• Cook for 7–10 minutes, or until the mussels open. Discard any unopened mussels. Remove the mussels; set aside and keep warm • Gradually add the butter to the wine mixture, stirring continuously. The sauce will thicken. • Return the mussels to the sauce and stir well to combine. • Divide evenly among four serving plates or bowls. • Serve hot.

- **1 cup (250 ml) white wine**
- **1 teaspoon saffron threads**
- **8 large tomatoes, diced**
- **2 pounds (1 kg) mussels, in shells, cleaned and beards removed**
- **1/2 cup (125 g) butter, cubed**

**Serves: 4**
**Preparation: 15 minutes**
**Cooking: 15 minutes**
**Level: 1**

# OYSTERS WITH BLACK BEAN DRESSING

Line a large steamer with parchment paper. Make holes in the paper so that the steam can penetrate. • To open the oysters, use a strong short knife or oyster shucker and insert it anywhere between the shells. Once the oyster is open, use the point of the knife to scrape the meat attached to the top shell into the bottom shell. Discard the top shell. • Place the oysters in the steamer in a single layer. • Combine the chiles, cilantro, black beans, and lime juice in a small bowl. • Spoon the sauce into the oyster shells and cover with a lid. • Place the steamer over a saucepan of boiling water. • Steam for 2 minutes. • Serve hot.

**24 oysters, in shells**
**3 small fresh, red chiles, seeded and finely sliced**
**2 tablespoons finely chopped fresh cilantro (coriander)**
**1 tablespoon fermented black beans, rinsed and roughly chopped**
**3 tablespoons (45 ml) freshly squeezed lime juice**

**Serves: 2–4**
**Preparation: 10 minutes**
**Cooking: 2 minutes**
**Level: 1**

■ ■ ■ *Fermented black beans, also known as Chinese black beans or salty black beans, are small black soybeans that have been preserved in salt. They are available in Asian specialty stores. If you can't get them, substitute with the same amount of Chinese black bean sauce, which is more widely available.*

# SCALLOP CEVICHE

Take the scallops off the shells. Reserve the shells. • Remove the white membrane from scallops using a small knife. • Place the scallops in a medium nonreactive bowl. • Add the lime juice, zest, chile, and cilantro. • Stir to combine well. • Cover and refrigerate for 1 hour, or until the scallops begin to turn from opaque to white. • Place the scallops back on the shells and drizzle the dressing in the bowl over the top. • Season with cracked pepper and serve.

**16 scallops, in half shells**
**8 limes, juiced + 1 tablespoon finely chopped lime zest**
**1 large green chile, seeded and finely diced**
**3 tablespoons finely chopped fresh cilantro (coriander)**
**Cracked pepper**

**Serves: 2**
**Preparation: 15 minutes + 1 hr to chill**
**Level: 1**

# SHRIMP AND PAPAYA SALAD



Combine the sesame oil and lime juice in a large bowl. • Dice the papaya into $^{3}/_{4}$-inch (2-cm) pieces and add to the dressing. • Add the shrimp and curly endive and toss well to combine. • Divide the salad evenly among four serving plates and serve.

- **$^{1}/_{4}$ cup (60 ml) Asian sesame oil**
- **$^{1}/_{4}$ cup (60 ml) freshly squeezed lime juice**
- **1 large papaya (pawpaw), peeled, halved and seeded**
- **$1^{1}/_{4}$ pounds (600 g) cooked shrimp (prawn), peeled and deveined**
- **3 cups (150 g) curly endive leaves, washed**

**Serves: 4**
**Preparation: 5 minutes**
**Level: 1**

# SHRIMP COCKTAIL

Combine the mayonnaise and lime juice in a large bowl. • Add the shrimp and mangoes and stir well to combine. • Roughly shred the lettuce and divide among four serving bowls. If preferred, use whole leaves. • Divide the shrimp mixture among the bowls on top of the lettuce and serve.

- **3/4 cup (180 ml) mayonnaise**
- **1/4 cup (60 ml) freshly squeezed lime juice**
- **1 1/2 pounds (750 g) cooked shrimp (prawn), peeled and deveined**
- **2 mangoes, peeled and diced**
- **1 small head romaine (cos) lettuce**

**Serves: 4**
**Preparation: 15 minutes**
**Level: 1**

# BLACK BEAN SQUID



Use a sharp knife to score the squid: make diagonal cuts ½-inch (1-cm) apart into the flesh in both directions. The cuts should just open the surface of flesh, not go all the way through. This will make a diamond pattern. • Cut the squid into 1½-inch (4-cm) pieces and set aside. • Heat the oil in a wok over medium-high heat. • Add the bell peppers and cook for 30 seconds. • Add the squid and scallions and cook for 1 minute, or until the squid begins to curl and change color. • Pour in the black bean sauce and bring to a simmer. • Toss well to combine. • Serve hot.

**2 pounds (1 kg) squid, cleaned and tentacles reserved**
**2 tablespoons (30 ml) Asian sesame oil**
**2 red bell peppers (capsicums), seeded and diced**
**4 scallions (spring onions), cut into 1-inch (2.5-cm) lengths**
**½ cup (125 ml) Chinese black bean sauce**

**Serves: 4**
**Preparation: 15–20 minutes**
**Cooking: 2–3 minutes**
**Level: 2**

■ ■ ■ *There are two ways to cook squid so that it doesn't become rubbery. You may either you cook it slowly over low heat for a long time, or sizzle it quickly over high heat for just a minute or two.*

# PAN-FRIED SALMON WITH GRAPEFRUIT SALAD

Combine the dill and 3 tablespoons (45 ml) of the oil in a small bowl. • Place a large frying pan on high heat. • Coat the salmon in the dill oil and place in the hot pan, skin side down. Cook two fillets at a time so that pan retains its heat. • Cook for 2–3 minutes on each side; the salmon should still be a little translucent inside. • Combine the watercress, grapefruit, reserved juice, and the remaining 1 tablespoon of oil in a medium bowl. • Divide the fish and salad evenly among four serving plates. • Serve hot.

**4 tablespoons finely chopped fresh dill**
**1/4 cup (60 ml) extra-virgin olive oil**
**4 (8-ounce/250 g) salmon fillets**
**3 cups (150 g) watercress sprigs**
**2 pink grapefruit, peeled and segmented, juice reserved**

**Serves: 4**
**Preparation: 10 minutes**
**Cooking: 8–12 minutes**
**Level: 1**

■ ■ ■ *If you live in Australia, substitute ocean trout for the salmon, if preferred.*

# BAKED SALMON WITH THYME POTATOES

Preheat the oven to 400°F (200°C/gas 6). • Put the potatoes in a large saucepan of salted boiling water. Cook for 3–4 minutes, or until just tender. Drain well. • Combine the potatoes, half the oil and half the thyme in a large ovenproof dish. • Mix gently to coat the potatoes with oil and bake for 25–30 minutes. • Pour the remaining oil into a large frying pan over high heat. • Cook the salmon fillets for 1 minute on each side. • Place the salmon on top of the potatoes, sprinkle with the capers, and bake for 8–10 minutes, or until the salmon is just cooked. • Divide the potatoes evenly among four serving plate and top with the salmon. • Serve hot.

**2 pounds (1 kg) potatoes, peeled and thickly sliced**
**1/3 cup (90 ml) extra-virgin olive oil**
**12 fresh thyme sprigs**
**4 (6-ounce/180-g) salmon fillets, skin removed**
**1/4 cup (50 g) salt-cured capers, rinsed**

**Serves: 4**
**Preparation: 5 minutes**
**Cooking: 40–45 minutes**
**Level: 1**

# RED WINE POACHED SALMON

Combine the wine and thyme in a large frying pan over medium heat and bring to a boil. • Reduce the heat to simmer, add the salmon, and cover. • Poach for 8–10 minutes, or until salmon is almost cooked through. • Baste with the wine occasionally if the salmon is not completely covered. • Remove the salmon using a slotted spoon; set aside and keep warm. • Increase the heat to high and boil the wine rapidly until reduced to 1/2 cup (125 ml). • Remove from the heat and gradually whisk in the butter. The sauce will thicken a little. • Meanwhile, bring a large saucepan of water to a boil. • Add the broccoli and cook for 3 minutes. • Divide the salmon and broccoli evenly among four serving plates. • Spoon the sauce over the salmon. • Serve hot.

**2 cups (500 ml) Pinot Noir wine**

**8 sprigs fresh thyme**

**4 (6-ounce/180-g) salmon fillets, skin removed**

**1/4 cup (60 g) salted butter, cubed**

**2 bunches broccoli, trimmed, broken into florets**

**Serves: 4**
**Preparation: 5 minutes**
**Cooking: 11–13 minutes**
**Level: 2**

# BAKED SEA BASS WITH CAPERS AND LEMON

Preheat the oven 350°F (180°C/gas 4). • Line a large baking sheet with aluminum foil. • Place the sea bass on the foil, sprinkle with the capers, and cover with the slices of lemon. • Cover with foil, so that fish is entirely encased and the juices will not spill out during cooking. • Bake for 12–15 minutes. • Combine the arugula and tomato in a medium bowl and toss to combine. • Divide the fish and salad evenly among four serving plates. • Serve hot.

- **4 (8-ounce/250 g) sea bass (barramundi) fillets or steaks**
- **2 lemons, thinly sliced, with peel**
- **2 tablespoons salt-cured capers, rinsed**
- **3 cups (150 g) arugula (rocket) leaves**
- **4 large tomatoes, diced**

**Serves: 4**
**Preparation: 5 minutes**
**Cooking: 12–15 minutes**
**Level: 1**

■ ■ ■ *You will need a large, firm-fleshed fish to make this recipe. Some good alternatives (depending on where you live) are red snapper, croaker, halibut, grouper, monkfish, trevally, hapuku, mako shark, or rockfish.*

# CRUMBED FISH WITH TARTAR SAUCE



Put the bread crumbs on a large plate or tray. • Press the fish fillets into the bread crumbs so that they are thoroughly coated; set aside. • Heat the oil in a large frying pan over medium heat. • Cook the fish for 3 minutes on each side, or until the flesh flakes easily and the crumbs are golden. • Place the fish and salad greens on four serving plates. Spoon the tartar sauce into four small bowls, one for each plate. • Serve hot.

- **1½ cups (90 g) fresh bread crumbs**
- **4 (8-ounce/250 g) fillets firm white fish, such as snapper, John Dory, whiting, blue-eye, cod, flounder, grouper, halibut**
- **½ cup (125 ml) canola oil**
- **3 cups (150 g) mixed salad greens**
- **¾ cup (180 ml) tartare sauce**

**Serves: 4**
**Preparation: 5 minutes**
**Cooking: 6 minutes**
**Level: 1**

# TUNA TARTARE

Remove the blood line and any bones from the tuna. • Dice the tuna into 3/4-inch (2-cm) cubes and place in a large bowl. • Dice the avocado to about the same size and add to the tuna. • Add the capers and lemon juice and gently stir to combine well. • Divide the tuna and watercress evenly among four serving plates and serve.

- **1 1/2 pounds (750 g) yellowfin tuna**
- **2 avocados, peeled, halved, and seeded**
- **3 cups (150 g) watercress sprigs**
- **2 tablespoons salt-cured capers, rinsed**
- **1/4 cup (60 ml) freshly squeezed lemon juice**

**Serves: 4**
**Preparation: 10 minutes**
**Level: 1**

# GRILLED TUNA WITH WATERMELON SALAD

Combine the watercress, watermelon, and 1 tablespoon (15 ml) of the oil in a medium bowl. • Toss to combine well and divide among four serving plates. • Heat a barbecue grill to medium-high heat. • Coat the tuna with the remaining 2 tablespoons of oil and cook for 2 minutes on each side; the tuna should still be pink inside. • Place the tuna on the salad and top with cracked pepper to taste. • Serve hot.

**1 cup (50 g) watercress sprigs**

**2 cups (400 g) cubed watermelon**

**3 tablespoons (45 ml) lemon-infused olive oil**

**4 (8-ounce/250-g) tuna steaks, cut about 1 inch (2.5 cm) thick**

**Cracked pepper**

Serves: 4
Preparation: 10 minutes
Cooking: 4 minutes
Level: 1

# CEVICHE WITH MANGO

Cut the fish into 3/4-inch (2-cm) pieces and put into a medium bowl. • Add the mango, chiles, lime juice, and zest and stir well to combine. • Cover the bowl and refrigerate for 1 hour, or until fish turns from opaque to white. • Season to taste with salt and serve.

**2 pounds (1 kg) skinless firm white fish fillets, such as flounder, snapper, grouper, cod, or trevalla**

**1 large mango, peeled and diced**

**3 small red chiles, seeded and finely chopped**

**8 limes, juiced + 1 tablespoon finely chopped lime zest**

**Sea salt**

Serves: 4
Preparation: 15 minutes + 1 hour to chill
Level: 1

# BARBECUED SARDINES

Combine the lemon juice, zest, and 2 tablespoons (30 ml) of the oil in a large bowl. • Add the sardines, toss to coat, and leave to marinate for 1 hour. • Preheat a barbecue grill to medium-high heat. • Cook the sardines for 2 minutes on each side, or until cooked through. • Combine the arugula, olives, and remaining 1 tablespoon of oil in a medium bowl. • Divide the salad and sardines evenly among four serving plates. • Serve hot.



**2 lemons, 1 juiced and zest removed, 1 cut into wedges**

**3 tablespoons (45 ml) rosemary-infused olive oil**

**8 large fresh sardines, cleaned and gutted**

**3 cups (150 g) arugula (rocket) leaves**

**1/2 cup (50 g) black olives**

**Serves: 4**
**Preparation: 10 minutes + 1 hour to marinate**
**Cooking: 4–5 minutes**
**Level: 1**

# STEAMED FISH WITH SHIITAKES AND BOK CHOY

Combine the mushrooms and oyster sauce in a medium frying pan over medium-low heat. • Cook for 3–4 minutes, until the mushrooms begin to soften. • Line a large steamer with parchment paper. Make holes in the paper so that the steam can penetrate. • Place the fish on top in a single layer and coat with the mushroom sauce. • Cover and place the steamer over a saucepan of boiling water. • Steam the fish for 6–7 minutes, until cooked through. • Meanwhile, bring a large saucepan of water to a boil. • Add the boy choy and cook for 2–3 minutes, or until softened. • Top the fish with chives and plate with the bok choy. Serve hot.

- **5 ounces (150 g) shiitake mushrooms, stems removed and caps thinly sliced**
- **3/4 cup (180 ml) Chinese oyster sauce**
- **4 (6-ounce/180-g) firm white fish fillets, such as red mullet, John Dory, sea bass, hapuku, cod, ling, flounder, pollack, monkfish, grouper, tilapia**
- **2 bunches baby bok choy, trimmed and cut into quarters lengthwise**
- **1 bunch chives, cut into 2-inch (5-cm) lengths**

**Serves: 4**
**Preparation: 5 minutes**
**Cooking: 10–15 minutes**
**Level: 1**

■ ■ ■ *Shiitake mushrooms are native to East Asia but are now cultivated around the globe. Their English name is taken from the Japanese. Shiitakes have a velvety texture and a deep, smoky flavor. The tough stems are not usually eaten. These mushrooms are also known as black forest mushrooms, winter mushrooms, or Chinese black mushrooms.*

# GRILLED SNAPPER WITH FRESH TOMATO SALSA

Preheat a barbecue grill or grill pan over medium-high heat. • Score the snapper with a sharp knife, making three cuts on each side. • Rub the fish with the olive oil. • Grill for 10 minutes on each side, or until the skin becomes crisp and the flesh flakes easily. (Cooking time will vary depending on the size of the fish.) • Mix the tomatoes, onion, and vinegar in a medium bowl. Spoon over the cooked fish. • Serve hot.

- **1 whole snapper, 4–6 pounds (2–3 kg), scaled, cleaned, and fins trimmed**
- **1/4 cup (60 ml) infused olive oil (chile or herb)**
- **1 1/4 pounds (600 g) cherry tomatoes, halved**
- **1 large red onion, diced**
- **1/4 cup (60 ml) balsamic vinegar**

Serves: 4
Preparation: 10 minutes
Cooking: 20 minutes
Level: 1

# BAKED FISH STEAKS WITH ROASTED TOMATOES

Preheat the oven to 400°F (200°C/gas 6). • Combine the tomatoes and olives in a medium baking dish and drizzle with half the oil. Bake for 5 minutes. • Add the fish and bake for 10–15 minutes, or until the flesh flakes easily. • Remove the fish and keep warm. • Stir the arugula through the roasted tomatoes and olives. Divide evenly among four serving dishes and place the fish on top. • Serve hot.

- **6 plum (roma) tomatoes, halved**
- **1/2 cup (50 g) black olives**
- **1/3 cup (90 ml) extra-virgin olive oil**
- **4 (8-ounce/250 g) firm white fish steaks, such as cod, snapper, ling, or warehou, cut about 3/4 inch (2 cm) thick**
- **2 cups (100 g) arugula (rocket) leaves**

**Serves:** 4
**Preparation:** 5 minutes
**Cooking:** 15–20 minutes
**Level:** 1

# JAPANESE-STYLE FISH

Mix the miso and mirin in a small bowl. • Rub the miso marinade over the fish and refrigerate for 2 hours. • Bring a large saucepan of water to a boil. • Add the rice and cook until tender, about 10–15 minutes. • Drain and set aside. • Preheat a grill pan over medium-high heat. • Cook the fish for 3 minutes on each side, or until the flesh flakes easily. • Divide the fish and rice evenly among four serving bowls or plates. Top with the pickled ginger. • Serve hot.

**1/4 cup (60 ml) miso**

**1/4 cup (60 ml) mirin (Japanese cooking wine)**

**8 (3-ounce/90 g) pieces firm white fish, such as snapper, John Dory, whiting, cod**

**1 1/2 cups (300 g) basmati rice**

**1/2 cup (100 g) pickled ginger**

**Serves: 4**
**Preparation: 10 minutes + 2 hours to marinate**
**Cooking: 20–25 minutes**
**Level: 1**

■ ■ ■ *Pickled ginger, also known as gari or sushoga (from the Japanese), is ginger preserved in rice vinegar, brine, or red wine. It is sweet and slightly spicy.*
*Mirin is a low-alcohol Japanese rice wine. It is not always easy to find, but you can make a reasonable substitute by bringing 1/4 cup (50 g) sugar to a boil with 2–3 tablespoons water. Let cool, then stir in about 2/3 cup (150 ml) good-quality sake.*

# STEAMED GINGER FISH WITH RICE

Bring a large saucepan of water to a boil. • Add the rice and cook until tender, about 10–15 minutes. • Drain and set aside. • Line a large steamer with parchment paper. Make holes in the paper so that the steam can penetrate. • Combine the ginger, lime juice, zest, and oyster sauce in a small bowl. • Coat the fish with ginger sauce. • Place the fish in the steamer and cook for 6–10 minutes, until the flesh flakes easily. • Divide the rice and fish evenly among four serving plates or bowls. • Serve hot, garnished with the extra lime.

- **1 1/2 cups (300 g) basmati rice**
- **4 (6-ounce/180-g) firm fish fillets, such as cod, trevally, halibut, flounder pollock, hapuku, grouper, or rockfish**
- **1 (2-inch/5-cm) piece ginger, peeled and cut into matchsticks**
- **1 lime, juiced and zest finely chopped, + 1 extra lime, quartered, to garnish**
- **1/4 cup (60 ml) Chinese oyster sauce**

**Serves: 4**
**Preparation: 10 minutes**
**Cooking: 20–25 minutes**
**Level: 1**

■ ■ ■ *Chinese oyster sauce is a thick, brown sauce made from a mixture of oysters, brine, and soy sauce. It is readily available in Asian food stores and supermarkets.*

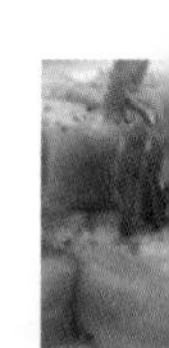

# CAJUN FISH WITH GRILLED LEMON

Brush the fish with 1/4 cup (60 g) of butter and coat in the Cajun spices. • Place a large frying pan over medium-high heat. • Drizzle with a little butter. • Cook the fish for 2 minutes on each side, or until flesh flakes easily. Add the remaining butter as you turn the fish. • Place a small frying pan over high heat. • Grill the lemons flesh side down for 1 minute, or until colored. • Serve the fish hot with the spinach and grilled lemon.

**4 (8-ounce/250-g) white fish fillets, such as cod, snapper, ling, or warehou**

**1/2 cup (125 g) butter, melted**

**2 tablespoons Cajun spice mix**

**3 cups (150 g) baby spinach leaves**

**2 lemons, halved**

**Serves: 4**
**Preparation: 5–10 minutes**
**Cooking: 5 minutes**
**Level: 1**

# BAKED SWORDFISH AND FENNEL

Preheat the oven to 375°F (190°C/gas 5). • Heat 2 tablespoons (30 ml) of the oil in a large frying pan over medium heat. • Add the fennel and cook for 5 minutes, or until soft. • Combine the swordfish, fennel, caperberries, and remaining 2 tablespoons of oil in a large baking dish. • Bake for 10 minutes. • Add the wine and bake for 5 more minutes, or until the fish is cooked through. • Serve hot, with the pan juices spooned over the top.

- **1/4 cup (60 ml) extra-virgin olive oil**
- **4 baby fennel bulbs, trimmed and thinly sliced**
- **4 (6-ounce/180-g) swordfish steaks**
- **1/3 cup (75 g) caperberries**
- **3/4 cup (180 ml) dry white wine**

**Serves: 4**
**Preparation: 5 minutes**
**Cooking: 20 minutes**
**Level: 1**

■ ■ ■ *Caperberries are not the same as capers although they come from the same plant. Capers are immature flower buds, harvested before they bloom. If left on the bush, the capers bloom and then mature into oval-shaped fruit, called caperberries.*

# CINNAMON POACHED MONKFISH

Preheat the oven to 325°F (170°C/gas 3). • Wrap each fish tail in two slices of prosciutto, securing with a toothpick. • Combine the fish stock and cinnamon sticks in a medium baking dish. • Add the wrapped fish, cover, and poach in the oven for 40–50 minutes, until the fish is cooked through. • Remove the toothpicks. • Meanwhile, add the potatoes to a large saucepan of salted boiling water. Cook for 4–5 minutes, or until tender. Drain well. • Divide the potatoes and fish evenly among four serving plates. • Serve hot.

**4 (6-ounce/180-g) monkfish tails or fillets**
**8 slices prosciutto (Parma ham)**
**3 cups (750 ml) fish stock**
**2 cinnamon sticks**
**1 pound (500 g) potatoes, peeled and sliced**

Serves: 4
Preparation: 10 minutes
Cooking: 40–45 minutes
Level: 1

# STEAMED FISH WITH GREEN BEANS AND PRESERVED LEMON

Line a large steamer with parchment paper. Make holes in the paper so that the steam can penetrate. • Place the fish in the steamer in a single layer and cover. • Place the steamer over a saucepan of boiling water. • Steam the fish for 6–7 minutes, until cooked through. • Meanwhile, bring a large saucepan of water to a boil. • Add the beans and cook for 3 minutes. Drain well and place in a medium bowl. • Add the preserved lemons and olive oil and toss to combine. • Divide the beans evenly among four serving plates. • Top with the fish and season with cracked pepper to taste. • Serve hot.

**4 (8-ounce/250-g) firm white fish fillets, such as grouper, hapuku, cod, ling, halibut, flounder, pollock, or monkfish**

**12 ounces (350 g) green beans, trimmed**

**2 preserved lemon quarters, rinsed and finely sliced**

**2 tablespoons (30 ml) extra-virgin olive oil**

**Cracked pepper**

**Serves: 4**
**Preparation: 5 minutes**
**Cooking: 10 minutes**
**Level: 1**

# PESTO FISH WITH ORANGE AND OLIVE SALAD



Heat a large nonstick frying pan over medium-high heat. • Coat the fish in the pesto and cook for 3 minutes on each side, or until the flesh flakes easily. • Combine the arugula, orange segments, and olives in a medium bowl. • Divide the salad and fish evenly among four serving plates. • Serve hot.

- **4 (8-ounce/250-g) firm white fish fillets, such as red mullet, John Dory, sea bass, hapuku, cod, ling, halibut, flounder, pollock, monkfish, grouper, rockfish, or tilapia**
- **1/2 cup (125 g) basil pesto**
- **3 cups (150 g) arugula (rocket) leaves**
- **4 oranges, peeled and segmented**
- **3/4 cup (75 g) black olives**

**Serves: 4**
**Preparation: 5 minutes**
**Cooking: 6 minutes**
**Level: 1**

# BAKED FISH WITH CANNELLINI BEANS

Preheat the oven to 350°F (180°C/gas 4). • Combine the beans, artichokes, marinade, and anchovies in a large baking dish. • Stir to combine well and bake for 35 minutes. • Place the fish in the baking dish and bake for 15–20 minutes, until cooked through. • Stir the parsley into the bean mixture and divide evenly among four serving plates. Top with the fish. • Serve hot.

- **1 (14-ounce/400-g) can cannellini beans, rinsed and drained**
- **8 ounces (250 g) marinated artichoke hearts, marinade reserved**
- **8 anchovy fillets, finely chopped**
- **4 (6-ounce/180-g) firm white fish fillets, such as red mullet, John Dory, sea bass, hapuku, cod, ling, halibut, flounder, pollack, monkfish, grouper, rockfish, or tilapia**
- **$^{1}/_{2}$ cup (50 g) fresh parsley leaves**

**Serves: 4**
**Preparation: 5 minutes**
**Cooking: 50–55 minutes**
**Level: 1**

# POACHED FLOUNDER WITH ASPARAGUS

Combine the stock, wine, and thyme in a large frying pan and bring to a boil. • Reduce the heat to a gentle simmer. • Meanwhile, bring a large saucepan of water to a boil.• Add the asparagus and cook for 2–3 minutes, or until tender. Drain and keep warm. • Poach the flounder fillets in the stock for 3–4 minutes, until the flesh flakes easily. • Divide the fish and asparagus among four serving dishes. Add a drizzle of the poaching liquid and serve hot.

**2 cups (500 ml) fish stock**

**1/2 cup (125 ml) white wine**

**8 lemon thyme sprigs**

**2 bunches asparagus, woody stems removed**

**4 (6-ounce/180-g) flounder fillets**

Serves: 4
Preparation: 5 minutes
Cooking: 6–7 minutes
Level: 1

# CHICKEN

# CHICKEN BAKED WITH FENNEL AND OLIVES

Preheat the oven to 350°F (180°C/gas 4). • Fry the chicken in 2 tablespoons of oil in a large frying pan over medium-high heat for 5 minutes, until browned all over. • Transfer the chicken to a baking dish. • Arrange the fennel and olives in the baking dish with the chicken. Sprinkle with the rosemary and drizzle with the remaining 1 tablespoon oil. • Bake for about 30 minutes, or until cooked through. • Serve hot.

- **4 chicken leg quarters**
- **3 tablespoons extra-virgin olive oil**
- **6 baby fennel, cut in half lengthwise**
- **1/2 cup (50 g) black olives, pitted (stoned)**
- **1 tablespoon coarsely chopped fresh rosemary**

**Serves: 4**
**Preparation: 5 minutes**
**Cooking: 35 minutes**
**Level: 1**

# GLAZED APRICOT CHICKEN

Preheat the oven to 350°F (180°C/gas 4). • Combine the apricots and juice, chicken stock, and apple cider vinegar in a medium saucepan and bring to a boil. • Arrange the chicken breasts in a baking dish in a single layer and pour in the apricot mixture. • Bake for 10 minutes. • Remove from the oven and baste with the juices. Bake for 15 minutes, basting the chicken every 5 minutes. • Remove the chicken from the oven and set aside. • Bring a large saucepan of salted water to a boil. • Add the rice and cook over medium heat for 10–15 minutes until tender. • Drain well. • Arrange the rice on serving plates, topped with the chicken and sauce. • Serve hot.

**1 (14-ounce/400-g) can apricot halves, with half the juice reserved**

**1 cup (250 ml) chicken stock**

**1 tablespoon apple cider vinegar**

**4 boneless, skinless chicken breasts**

**1½ cups (300 g) basmati rice**

**Serves: 4**
**Preparation: 10 minutes**
**Cooking: 35–40 minutes**
**Level: 1**

# CHICKEN COUSCOUS WITH PRESERVED LEMON

Combine the stock and oregano in a large saucepan and bring to a boil. • Add the chicken and decrease the heat to low. • Poach the chicken for 10–15 minutes, until cooked through. • Remove the chicken, cover, and keep warm. • Combine the couscous and preserved lemon in a medium bowl. Pour the hot stock over the couscous. • Cover the bowl with plastic wrap (cling film) and let stand for 10 minutes, until the couscous has completely absorbed the liquid. • Thinly slice the chicken and mix into the couscous. • Serve hot.

**$1^3/4$ cups (430 ml) chicken stock**
**3 tablespoons fresh oregano leaves**
**4 boneless, skinless chicken breasts**
**$1^1/2$ cups (300 g) instant couscous**
**3 preserved lemon quarters, thinly sliced**

Serves: 4
Preparation: 10 minutes + 10 minutes to stand
Cooking: 10–15 minutes
Level: 1

# POACHED COCONUT CHICKEN

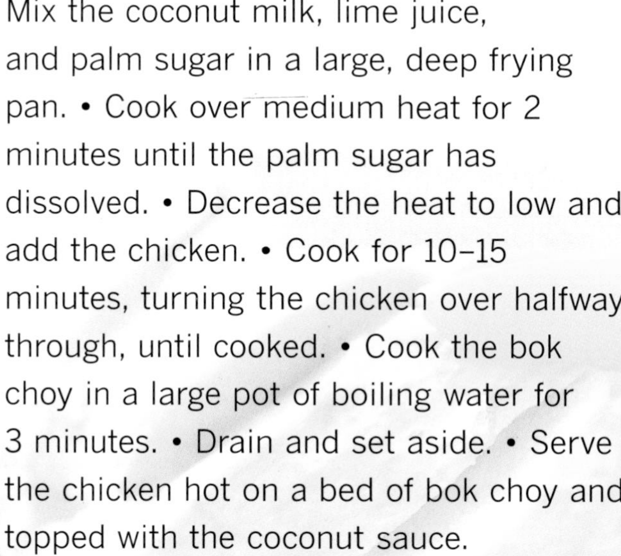

Mix the coconut milk, lime juice, and palm sugar in a large, deep frying pan. • Cook over medium heat for 2 minutes until the palm sugar has dissolved. • Decrease the heat to low and add the chicken. • Cook for 10–15 minutes, turning the chicken over halfway through, until cooked. • Cook the bok choy in a large pot of boiling water for 3 minutes. • Drain and set aside. • Serve the chicken hot on a bed of bok choy and topped with the coconut sauce.

- **1 2/3 cups (400 ml) coconut milk**
- **2 tablespoons freshly squeezed lime juice**
- **1 1/2 tablespoons palm sugar or coconut sugar (or substitute raw sugar)**
- **4 boneless, skinless chicken breasts**
- **8 baby bok choy, halved**

**Serves: 4**
**Preparation: 10 minutes**
**Cooking: 15–20 minutes**
**Level: 1**

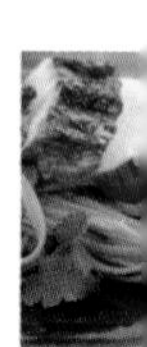

# CHICKEN AND SUGAR SNAP SALAD

Cook the sugar snap peas in boiling water for 2 minutes. • Drain and rinse under ice-cold water to stop the cooking process. • Combine the sugar snap peas, spinach, and mint in a large bowl. Toss well. • Divide the salad among four serving plates. • Top with the chicken and drizzle with the coconut milk. • Serve at room temperature.

**12 ounces (350 g) sugar snap peas, trimmed**

**3 cups (150 g) baby spinach leaves**

**16 fresh mint leaves**

**4 cooked, smoked boneless chicken breasts, thinly sliced**

**1/3 cup (90 ml) coconut milk**

Serves: 4
Preparation: 10 minutes
Cooking: 2 minutes
Level: 1

# TERIYAKI CHICKEN WINGS

Put the chicken wings in a large bowl and cover with the teriyaki sauce. Cover with plastic wrap (cling film) and refrigerate for 1 hour. • Combine the tomatoes and cilantro in a medium bowl and mix well. • Bring a large saucepan of salted water to a boil. • Add the rice and cook over medium heat for 10–15 minutes until tender. • Drain well and keep warm. • Place a grill pan over medium-high heat. • Grill the chicken for 5 minutes on each side until cooked through. • Serve the chicken hot with the tomatoes and rice.

**20 chicken wings**

**3/4 cup (180 ml) teriyaki sauce**

**6 tomatoes, coarsely chopped**

**3 tablespoons fresh cilantro (coriander) leaves**

**1 1/2 cups (300 g) basmati rice**

**Serves: 4**
**Preparation: 10 minutes + 1 hour to marinate**
**Cooking: 20–25 minutes**
**Level: 1**

# SPICY SWEET CHICKEN

Coat the chicken with the honey and sambal oelek in a large bowl. • Cover with plastic wrap (cling film) and refrigerate for 1 hour. • Mix the spinach and tomatoes in a medium bowl. • Place a grill pan over medium-high heat. • Grill the chicken for 5 minutes on each side, until cooked through. • Serve the chicken hot with the salad.

**4 boneless, skinless chicken breasts**
**1/2 cup (125 ml) honey**
**1/4 cup (60 ml) sambal oelek**
**3 cups (150 g) baby spinach leaves**
**8 ounces (250 g) cherry tomatoes, halved**

**Serves: 4**
**Preparation: 10 minutes + 1 hour to marinate**
**Cooking: 10 minutes**
**Level: 1**

■ ■ ■ *Sambal oelek is a very spicy sauce made from chile peppers. Used in Indonesia and Malaysia as a condiment and available online, it can be replaced with minced fresh peppers.*

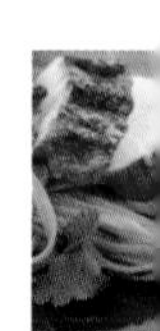

# CHICKEN WITH GRILLED FIG SALAD

Place a grill pan over medium-high heat. • Brush the chicken and figs with a little of the oil marinating the feta. • Grill the chicken for 5 minutes on each side, until cooked through. • Mix the arugula, feta, and orange zest and juice in a medium bowl. • Grill the figs for 2 minutes on each side until slightly softened. • Add the figs to the salad and toss well. • Thinly slice the chicken and add to the salad. • Serve at room temperature.

- **4 boneless, skinless chicken breasts**
- **4 fresh figs, cut in half lengthwise**
- **5 ounces (150 g) marinated feta, with oil**
- **3 cups (150 g) arugula (rocket) leaves**
- **Finely shredded zest and juice of 1 orange**

**Serves: 4**
**Preparation: 10 minutes**
**Cooking: 14 minutes**
**Level: 1**

# TANDOORI DRUMSTICKS

Use a sharp knife to make deep cuts all over the drumsticks. • Mix the yogurt, tandoori paste, and lemon juice in a large bowl. • Coat the drumsticks with the mixture. Cover with plastic wrap (cling film) and refrigerate for 1 hour. • Place a grill pan over medium-high heat. • Grill the drumsticks for 15 minutes, turning them often, until cooked through. • Serve the drumsticks hot with the arugula.

- **8 chicken drumsticks**
- **2/3 cup (150 ml) plain yogurt**
- **3 tablespoons tandoori paste**
- **Freshly squeezed juice of 1 lemon**
- **3 cups (150 g) arugula (rocket) leaves**

**Serves: 4**
**Preparation: 5 minutes + 1 hour to marinate**
**Cooking: 15 minutes**
**Level: 1**

■ ■ ■ *Tandoori paste is a bright red spice mixture made with garlic, ginger, cardamom, cumin, and many other spices. It is available online and wherever Indian foods are sold.*

# ORANGE-GLAZED CHICKEN WITH COUSCOUS

Mix the orange juice and honey in a large bowl. • Use a sharp knife to score the chicken skin, making diagonal cuts to form a diamond pattern and making sure that you don't cut into the flesh. • Coat the chicken with the orange mixture. Cover with plastic wrap (cling film) and refrigerate for 1 hour. • Put the couscous in a medium bowl. Add the chicken stock and orange zest. • Cover the bowl with plastic wrap and let stand for 10 minutes, until the couscous has completely absorbed the liquid. • Fluff up the couscous with a fork. • Place a grill pan over medium-high heat. • Grill the chicken for 5 minutes on each side, until cooked through. • Let rest in a warm place for 5 minutes. • Slice the chicken and serve hot on a bed of the couscous.

**Finely shredded zest and juice of 2 oranges**
**2 tablespoons honey**
**4 boneless chicken breasts, with skin on**
**1½ cups (300 g) instant couscous**
**1½ cups (375 ml) chicken stock, heated**

Serves: 4
Preparation: 25 minutes + 1 hour to marinate + 15 minutes to stand
Cooking: 10 minutes
Level: 1

# BALSAMIC CHICKEN WITH ROASTED TOMATOES

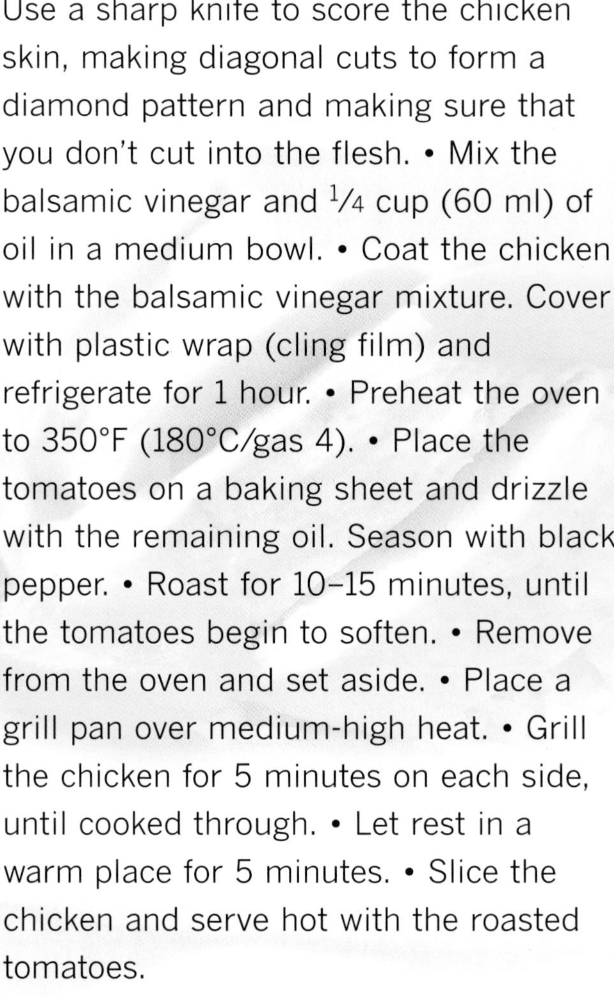

Use a sharp knife to score the chicken skin, making diagonal cuts to form a diamond pattern and making sure that you don't cut into the flesh. • Mix the balsamic vinegar and 1/4 cup (60 ml) of oil in a medium bowl. • Coat the chicken with the balsamic vinegar mixture. Cover with plastic wrap (cling film) and refrigerate for 1 hour. • Preheat the oven to 350°F (180°C/gas 4). • Place the tomatoes on a baking sheet and drizzle with the remaining oil. Season with black pepper. • Roast for 10–15 minutes, until the tomatoes begin to soften. • Remove from the oven and set aside. • Place a grill pan over medium-high heat. • Grill the chicken for 5 minutes on each side, until cooked through. • Let rest in a warm place for 5 minutes. • Slice the chicken and serve hot with the roasted tomatoes.

**4** **boneless chicken breasts, with skin on**
**1/2** **cup (125 ml) balsamic vinegar**
**1/3** **cup (90 ml) extra-virgin olive oil**
**16** **cherry tomatoes**
**Freshly ground black pepper**

**Serves: 4**
**Preparation: 10 minutes + 1 hour to marinate + 5 minutes to stand**
**Cooking: 20–25 minutes**
**Level: 1**

# SPICY CHICKEN WITH SOY NOODLES

Use a sharp knife to score the chicken skin, making diagonal cuts to form a diamond pattern and making sure that you don't cut into the flesh. • Coat the chicken in the five-spice powder and 2 tablespoons of the soy sauce in a medium bowl. Cover with plastic wrap (cling film) and refrigerate for 1 hour. • Cook the soba noodles in a large pot of salted boiling water for about 5 minutes, or until al dente. • Drain and rinse under cold running water. • Place the noodles in a large bowl. Mix in the cilantro and the remaining soy sauce. Set aside. • Place a grill pan over medium-high heat. • Grill the chicken for 5 minutes on each side until cooked through. • Let rest in a warm place for 5 minutes. • Slice the chicken and serve hot with the noodles.

**4 boneless chicken breasts, with skin on**
**2 tablespoons Chinese five-spice powder**
**1/3 cup (90 ml) soy sauce**
**14 ounces (400 g) dried soba noodles (see page 348)**
**3 tablespoons fresh cilantro (coriander) leaves**

**Serves: 4**
**Preparation: 10 minutes + 1 hour to marinate + 5 minutes to stand**
**Cooking: 15 minutes**
**Level: 1**

485

# LIME AND CILANTRO CHICKEN

Mix 2 tablespoons of the cilantro, the sesame oil, and lime zest and juice in a large bowl. • Coat the chicken with the lime mixture. Cover with plastic wrap (cling film) and refrigerate for 1 hour. • Bring a large saucepan of salted water to a boil. • Add the rice and cook over medium heat for 10–15 minutes until tender. • Drain well and keep warm. • Place a grill pan over medium-high heat. • Grill the chicken for 5 minutes on each side, until cooked through. • Let rest in a warm place for 5 minutes. • Slice the chicken and arrange on top of the rice. • Garnish with the remaining 2 tablespoons cilantro leaves and serve hot.

**4 tablespoons fresh cilantro (coriander) leaves**

**2 tablespoons Asian sesame oil**

**Finely grated zest and juice of 4 limes**

**4 boneless, skinless chicken breasts**

**$1^1/2$ cups (300 g) jasmine rice**

Serves: 4
Preparation: 10 minutes + 1 hour to marinate + 5 minutes to stand
Cooking: 20–25 minutes
Level: 1

■ ■ ■ *Limes are a citrus fruit thought to be native to Southeast Asia. In many Asian cuisines they occupy the place that the lemon fills in Mediterranean and other Western cuisines. Introduced to the Americas by the Spanish, limes grow well in the warm climates of Mexico and Central America and are of major importance in those cuisines. Green-skinned limes are smaller than most species of lemon, and they are slightly more acidic in flavor. Like all citrus fruits, limes are an excellent source of vitamin C.*

# MEDITERRANEAN CHICKEN KIEV



Mix the feta and tapenade in a small bowl. • Make a single cut in the chicken breasts to create a pocket and stuff with the feta mixture. Secure with toothpicks. • Place a large nonstick frying pan over medium heat. • Cook the chicken, 10–12 minutes, until golden brown on the outside and cooked through. • Place the arugula in a medium bowl and drizzle with the balsamic vinegar. • Slice the chicken and serve hot with the arugula.

- **4 ounces (125 g) feta cheese, crumbled**
- **1/4 cup (60 ml) olive tapenade**
- **4 boneless, skinless chicken breasts**
- **3 cups (150 g) arugula (rocket) leaves**
- **1/4 cup (60 ml) balsamic vinegar**

**Serves: 4**
**Preparation: 10 minutes**
**Cooking: 10–12 minutes**
**Level: 1**

■ ■ ■ *The original recipe for chicken Kiev comes from the Ukraine and consists of a boned chicken breast wrapped around herbed butter, coated with bread crumbs, then pan-fried. This is a lighter, Mediterranean version of this classic dish.*

# SUN-DRIED TOMATO CHICKEN WITH SPINACH

Coat the chicken with the pesto in a large bowl. Cover with plastic wrap (cling film) and refrigerate for 1 hour. • Dry-fry the pancetta in a medium saucepan over medium heat for 3 minutes until crispy. • Remove and set aside. • Pour in the cream and bring to a boil. Decrease the heat and simmer over low heat until the cream has reduced by half. • Meanwhile, place a grill pan over medium-high heat. • Grill the chicken for 5 minutes on each side until cooked through. • Let rest in a warm place for 5 minutes. • Add the spinach to the cream and cook until wilted. • Stir in the pancetta. • Serve the chicken hot with the creamy spinach.

- **4** **boneless, skinless chicken breasts**
- **1/3** **cup (90 ml) sun-dried tomato pesto**
- **12** **slices pancetta**
- **2** **cups (500 ml) light (single) cream**
- **6** **cups (300 g) baby spinach leaves**

**Serves: 4**
**Preparation: 10 minutes + 1 hour to marinate + 5 minutes to stand**
**Cooking: 20 minutes**
**Level: 1**

# THYME ROASTED CHICKEN WITH NEW POTATOES

Preheat the oven to 350°F (180°C/gas 4). • Brush the oil over and inside the cavity of the chicken and sprinkle with the thyme. Season with salt and place in a large baking dish. Cover with aluminum foil. • Bake for 1 hour. • Parboil the potatoes in boiling water for 5 minutes. Drain well and add to the baking dish with the chicken. • Bake, uncovered, for about 30 minutes, until the chicken juices run clear and the potatoes are cooked. • Serve the chicken hot with the potatoes.

- **1/4 cup (60 ml) extra-virgin olive oil**
- **1 (3-pound/1.5-kg) chicken**
- **5 tablespoons fresh lemon thyme leaves**
- **1 tablespoon coarse salt**
- **1 1/4 pounds (550 g) new potatoes**

**Serves: 4**
**Preparation: 10 minutes**
**Cooking: 1 hour 35 minutes**
**Level: 1**

# RED THAI CHICKEN

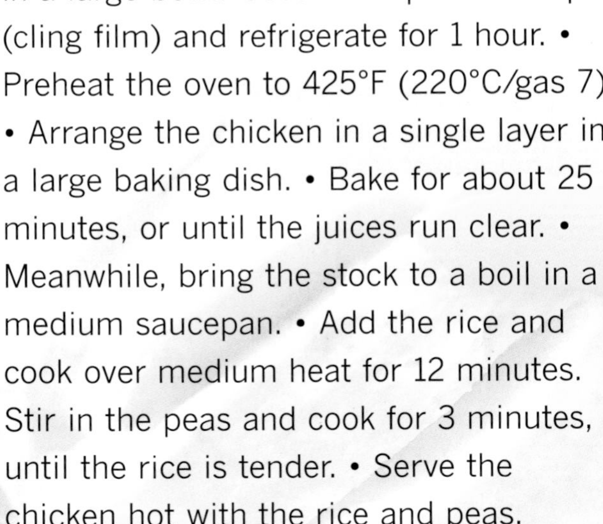

Coat the chicken with the red curry paste in a large bowl. Cover with plastic wrap (cling film) and refrigerate for 1 hour. • Preheat the oven to 425°F (220°C/gas 7). • Arrange the chicken in a single layer in a large baking dish. • Bake for about 25 minutes, or until the juices run clear. • Meanwhile, bring the stock to a boil in a medium saucepan. • Add the rice and cook over medium heat for 12 minutes. Stir in the peas and cook for 3 minutes, until the rice is tender. • Serve the chicken hot with the rice and peas.

**4 chicken leg quarters**

**1/4 cup (60 ml) Thai red curry paste**

**2 cups (500 ml) chicken stock**

**1 1/2 cups (300 g) basmati rice**

**1 cup (125 g) frozen peas**

**Serves: 4**

**Preparation: 5 minutes + 1 hour to marinate**

**Cooking: 40 minutes**

**Level: 1**

# TOMATO AND TARRAGON CHICKEN



Preheat the oven to 350°F (180°C/gas 4). • Combine the chicken, tomatoes, onions, olives, and tarragon in a large baking dish. • Bake for 30 minutes, until the chicken is cooked through. • Serve hot.

**4 chicken leg quarters**

**3½ cups (875 g) peeled and chopped tomatoes, with juice**

**2 red onions, thinly sliced**

**½ cup (50 g) black olives**

**2 tablespoons fresh tarragon leaves**

**Serves: 4**
**Preparation: 5 minutes**
**Cooking: 30 minutes**
**Level: 1**

# CRISPY CORIANDER CHICKEN



Preheat the oven to 400°F (200°C/ gas 6). • Toast the coriander seeds in a small frying pan over high heat for 2 minutes until aromatic. • Grind the coriander seeds with the salt with a mortar and pestle. • Add the sesame oil and set aside. • Arrange the chicken in a single layer in a large baking dish and coat with the coriander seed mixture. Make 3–4 slashes in the skin with a sharp knife. • Bake for 30 minutes, until the chicken is cooked through. • Cook the green beans in boiling water for 3 minutes until tender. Drain well. • Serve the chicken hot with the green beans.

**$1\frac{1}{2}$ tablespoons coriander seeds**
**2 teaspoons salt**
**2 tablespoons Asian sesame oil**
**4 chicken leg quarters**
**12 ounces (350 g) green beans**

**Serves:** 4
**Preparation:** 10 minutes
**Cooking:** 35 minutes
**Level:** 1

# SATAY CHICKEN PIE

Preheat the oven to 425°F (220°C/gas 7). • Cook the chicken, onions, and bell peppers in a large frying pan over medium heat for 3 minutes. • Add the satay sauce and cook for 2 minutes. • Pour the mixture into an 8-inch (20-cm) pie dish. Trim the pastry to fit the dish. • Brush the edges of the pie dish with water and place the puff pastry sheet on top. • Press the edges down firmly to seal. Decorate the top with the remaining pastry scraps. • Brush with a little water and prick all over with a fork. • Bake for 25–30 minutes, until golden brown. • Serve hot.

**3 boneless, skinless chicken breasts, cut into small pieces**

**2 onions, thinly sliced**

**2 red bell peppers (capsicums), seeded and diced**

**1 cup (250 ml) satay sauce (see page 352)**

**1 sheet puff pastry**

**Serves: 4**
**Preparation: 15 minutes**
**Cooking: 30–35 minutes**
**Level: 1**

# CAJUN CHICKEN KEBABS

Mix the oil and Cajun spice mix in a large bowl. • Coat the chicken with the spice mixture. Cover with plastic wrap (cling film) and chill for 1 hour. • Carefully thread the chicken onto metal skewers and set aside. • Bring a large saucepan of salted water to a boil. • Add the rice and cook over medium heat for 12 minutes. • Add the kidney beans and cook for 3 minutes until the rice is tender. • Drain well. • Place a grill pan over medium-high heat. • Grill the kebabs for 5 minutes on each side until cooked through. • Serve the kebabs hot with the rice and kidney beans.

**3 tablespoons extra-virgin olive oil**
**2 tablespoons Cajun spice mix**
**6 boneless, skinless chicken breasts, cut into small pieces**
**1½ cups (300 g) long-grain rice**
**4 cups (400 g) canned kidney beans, drained**

Serves: 4
Preparation: 15 minutes + 1 hour to marinate
Cooking: 25 minutes
Level: 1

# BAKED CHICKEN BREASTS WITH CHERRY TOMATOES

Preheat the oven to 350°F (180°C/gas 4). • Lightly pound the chicken with a meat tenderizer so that it is thin and of even thickness. • Place three sage leaves on each piece of chicken. Cover with the prosciutto and secure with a toothpick. • Place a nonstick frying pan over medium-high heat. • Cook the chicken for 3 minutes on each side until lightly browned. • Arrange the chicken in a single layer in a baking pan, Top with the tomatoes. • Bake for 10–15 minutes, until the tomatoes are softened and the chicken is cooked through. • Slice the chicken and serve hot with the arugula and tomatoes.

**4 boneless, skinless chicken breasts**

**12 leaves fresh sage**

**1 slices prosciutto (Parma ham)**

**1 pound (500 g) cherry tomatoes**

**3 cups (150 g) arugula (rocket) leaves**

Serves: 4
Preparation: 15 minutes
Cooking: 16–21 minutes
Level: 1

# CHICKEN WITH PUY LENTILS

Cover the lentils with cold water in a medium saucepan. • Bring to a boil. Decrease the heat and simmer over low heat for 15–20 minutes, until tender. • Drain and set aside. • Sauté the chicken with the lemon zest in 2 tablespoons of oil over medium heat for 5 minutes on each side, until cooked through. • Set aside and keep warm. • Heat the remaining oil in a large frying pan. • Add the lentils, oregano, and lemon juice. Cook for 3 minutes. • Serve the chicken hot with the lentils.

**1 2/3 cups (160 g) Puy lentils, soaked overnight and rinsed**
**4 boneless, skinless chicken breasts**
**Finely shredded zest and juice of 2 lemons**
**1/3 cup (90 ml) extra-virgin olive oil**
**4 tablespoons fresh oregano leaves**

**Serves: 4**
**Preparation: 10 minutes**
**Cooking: 28–33 minutes**
**Level: 1**

■ ■ ■ *Puy lentils come from Le Puy, in France. They have a unique peppery flavor and hold their shape well during cooking.*

# CHICKEN AND PESTO ORZO

Cook the orzo in a large pot of salted boiling water until al dente. • Mix the chicken, pesto, and lemon zest in a medium bowl. • Place a large nonstick frying pan over medium-high heat. • Cook the chicken for 4 minutes, until cooked through. • Add the tomatoes and lemon juice. • Drain the orzo and add to the pan with the sauce. • Toss well and serve hot.

- **1 pound (500 g) orzo (risoni)**
- **3 boneless, skinless chicken breasts, cut into thin strips**
- **1/3 cup (90 ml) basil pesto**
- **Grated zest and juice of 1 lemon**
- **6 tomatoes, coarsely chopped**

**Serves: 4**
**Preparation: 10 minutes**
**Cooking: 15 minutes**
**Level: 1**

# CUMIN CHICKEN KEBABS

Soak twelve bamboo skewers in cold water for 30 minutes so that they don't burn. Combine the oil and cumin in a large bowl. • Coat the chicken with the cumin mixture. Cover with plastic wrap (cling film) and refrigerate for 1 hour. • Carefully thread the chicken onto the skewers and set aside. • Place a grill pan over medium-high heat. • Grill the chicken for 5 minutes on each side until cooked through. • Serve the chicken hot with the salad greens and yogurt.

**3 tablespoons extra-virgin olive oil**

**2 tablespoons ground cumin**

**6 boneless, skinless chicken breasts, cut into small pieces**

**3 cups (150 g) mixed salad greens**

**1 cup (250 ml) plain yogurt**

Serves: 4–6
Preparation: 40 minutes + 1 hour to marinate
Cooking: 10 minutes
Level: 1

# PORK, LAMB, AND BEEF

# BAKED PORK CUTLETS WITH ZUCCHINI

Mix the lemon juice, oil, and olives in a small bowl. • Pour the mixture over the pork in a large bowl. Cover with plastic wrap (cling film) and refrigerate for 1 hour. • Preheat the oven to 400°F (200°C/gas 6). • Place a large nonstick frying pan over medium-high heat. • Cook the pork for 2 minutes on each side, until browned. • Transfer the pork to a large baking dish and add the zucchini and the marinade. • Bake for 15–20 minutes, turning the cutlets halfway through, until the pork and zucchini are tender. • Serve hot with the lemon quarters.

- **3 lemons, 1 juiced and 2 cut into quarters**
- **1/4 cup (60 ml) rosemary-infused olive oil**
- **1/2 cup (50 g) black olives**
- **4 bone-in pork cutlets, cut about 3/4 inch (2 cm) thick**
- **6 zucchini (courgettes), cut in half lengthwise**

**Serves: 4**
**Preparation: 5 minutes + 1 hour to marinate**
**Cooking: 20–25 minutes**
**Level: 1**

# HOISIN PORK WITH MANGO SALSA

Place the pork in a large bowl and cover with the hoisin sauce. Cover with plastic wrap (cling film) and refrigerate for 1 hour. • Preheat the oven to 375°F (190°C/gas 5). • Place a large nonstick frying pan over medium-high heat. • Cook the pork for 2 minutes on each side, until browned. • Transfer the pork to a large baking dish. • Bake for 15–20 minutes, until tender. • Remove from the oven and let rest for 5 minutes. • Mix the mangoes, cilantro, and chile peppers in a medium bowl. • Slice the pork and serve hot with the salsa.

- **3 pork fillets (about 12 ounces/350 g each)**
- **3/4 cup (180 ml) hoisin sauce**
- **2 large mangoes, cut into small cubes**
- **3 tablespoons fresh cilantro (coriander) leaves**
- **1 large fresh chile pepper, seeded and very thinly sliced**

**Serves: 4–6**
**Preparation: 10 minutes + 1 hour to marinate + 5 minutes to rest**
**Cooking: 20–25 minutes**
**Level: 1**

# PORK WRAPPED IN PROSCIUTTO

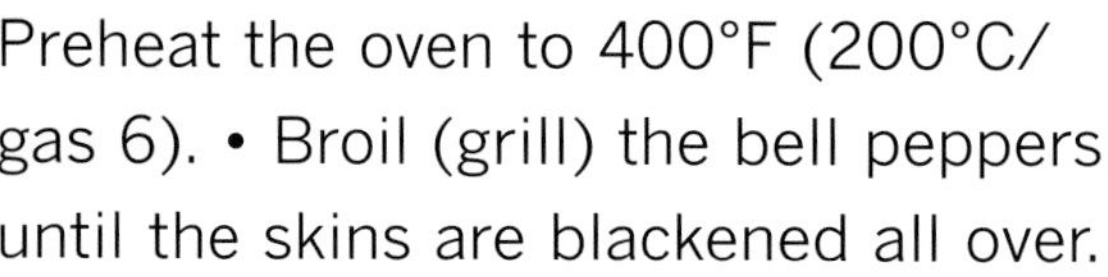

Preheat the oven to 400°F (200°C/ gas 6). • Broil (grill) the bell peppers until the skins are blackened all over. • Wrap them in a paper bag for 5 minutes, then remove the skins and seeds. Slice into strips. • Arrange three sage leaves on top of each pork fillet and wrap two slices of prosciutto around it. Secure with a toothpick. • Fry the pork in 2 tablespoons of oil in a large frying pan over medium-high heat for 2 minutes on each side, until browned. • Transfer the pork and juices to a large baking dish. • Bake for 15–20 minutes, until tender. • Heat the remaining oil in a large frying pan over low heat. • Add the bell peppers and cook for 1 minute. • Remove the pork from the oven and let rest for 5 minutes. • Slice the pork thickly and serve hot with the bell peppers.

**4 red bell peppers (capsicums)**
**12 fresh sage leaves**
**8 slices prosciutto (Parma ham)**
**3 pork fillets (about 12 ounces/350 g each)**
**1/4 cup (60 ml) extra-virgin olive oil**

**Serves: 6–8**
**Preparation: 15 minutes + 5 minutes to rest**
**Cooking: 25 minutes**
**Level: 1**

# TERIYAKI PORK WITH ASIAN GREENS

Place the pork in a large bowl and cover with the teriyaki sauce. Cover with plastic wrap (cling film) and refrigerate for 1 hour. • Preheat the oven to 375°F (190°C/gas 5). • Place a large nonstick frying pan over medium-high heat. • Cook the pork for 2 minutes on each side until browned. • Transfer the pork to a large baking dish. • Bake for 15–20 minutes until tender. • Remove from the oven and let rest for 5 minutes. • Cook the choy sum in a large saucepan of boiling water for 1 minute. • Add the bok choy and cook for 1–2 minutes, until both vegetables are tender. • Drain well and return to the pan. Add the sesame seeds and toss well. • Slice the pork thickly and serve hot with the Asian greens.

**3 pork fillets (about 12 ounces/350 g each)**

**3/4 cup (180 ml) teriyaki sauce**

**1 bunch choy sum, trimmed**

**2 bunches baby bok choy, cut in half lengthwise**

**3 tablespoons sesame seeds**

**Serves: 4–6**
**Preparation: 10 minutes + 1 hour to chill + 5 minutes to rest**
**Cooking: 15–18 minutes**
**Level: 1**

■ ■ ■ *Choy sum, also known as Chinese flowering cabbage, is a member of the cabbage family. Use all bok choy or replace with Swiss chard (silver beet), if preferred.*

# PORK STEAKS WITH BAKED APPLES

Preheat the oven to 350°F (180°C/gas 4). • Arrange the apple slices in a single layer in a large baking dish and drizzle with the maple syrup. • Fry the pork in 2 tablespoons of oil in a large frying pan over medium-high heat on each side for 2 minutes, until browned. • Remove from the pan and arrange on top of the apples. Drizzle with the remaining 2 tablespoons of oil. • Bake for 12–14 minutes, until the pork is tender and the apples have softened. • Arrange the pork on a bed of the apples on individual serving plates. Sprinkle with the walnuts, drizzle with the pan juices, and serve hot.

- **4 apples, cored and sliced into rounds**
- **3 tablespoons pure maple syrup**
- **4 pork loin steaks, cut about 3/4 inch (2 cm) thick**
- **1/4 cup (60 ml) extra-virgin olive oil**
- **3/4 cup (120 g) walnuts, toasted**

**Serves: 4**
**Preparation: 10 minutes**
**Cooking: 16–18 minutes**
**Level: 1**

# SPICED PORK WITH CABBAGE

Sprinkle the pork with the five-spice powder. • Fry the pork in 3 tablespoons of the oil in a large frying pan over medium-high heat for 5–6 minutes on each side, until tender and cooked to your liking. • Remove from the pan and let rest while you prepare the vegetables. • Heat the remaining 1 tablespoon of oil in a medium saucepan over low heat. • Add the onion and cook for 3 minutes. • Add the cabbage and cook for 4 minutes until wilted. • Slice the pork thickly and serve hot on a bed of the cabbage.

**3 pork fillets (about 12 ounces/350 g each)**

**2 tablespoons five-spice powder**

**1/4 cup (60 ml) Asian sesame oil**

**1 onion, thinly sliced**

**1/2 Savoy cabbage, cored and finely shredded**

Serves: 4–6
Preparation: 10 minutes
Cooking: 15 minutes
Level: 1

# PORK WITH ORANGE AND WATERCRESS SALAD

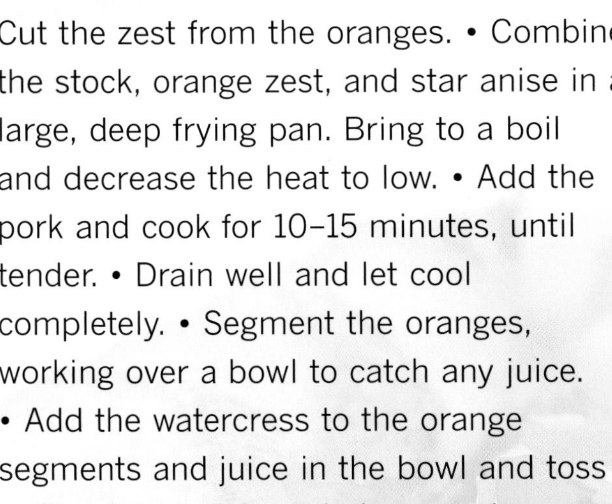

Cut the zest from the oranges. • Combine the stock, orange zest, and star anise in a large, deep frying pan. Bring to a boil and decrease the heat to low. • Add the pork and cook for 10–15 minutes, until tender. • Drain well and let cool completely. • Segment the oranges, working over a bowl to catch any juice. • Add the watercress to the orange segments and juice in the bowl and toss well. • Arrange the salad on serving plates. Slice the pork and place on top of the salad. • Serve at room temperature.

- **3 oranges**
- **2 cups (500 ml) chicken stock**
- **8 star anise**
- **3 pork fillets (about 12 ounces/350 g each)**
- **3 cups (150 g) watercress**

**Serves:** 4–6
**Preparation:** 10 minutes
**Cooking:** 10–15 minutes
**Level:** 1

# BAKED PORK CUTLETS WITH FENNEL

Preheat the oven to 400°F (200°C/ gas 6). • Cook the fennel in 2 tablespoons of the oil in a large frying pan over medium heat for about 5 minutes, or until slightly softened. • Transfer the fennel to a large baking dish. Add the tomatoes and thyme and mix well. • Fry the pork in the remaining 2 tablespoons of oil in a large frying pan over medium-high heat for 2 minutes on each side, until browned. • Transfer the pork to the baking dish with the fennel and tomatoes. • Cover with aluminum foil. • Bake for 20–25 minutes, until the pork and fennel are tender. • Serve hot.

- **2 bulbs fennel, thinly sliced**
- **1/4 cup (60 ml) extra-virgin olive oil**
- **3 1/4 cups (800 g) peeled and chopped tomatoes, with juice**
- **10 sprigs fresh thyme**
- **4 bone-in pork cutlets, cut 1/2 inch (1.5 cm) thick**

**Serves: 4**
**Preparation: 5 minutes**
**Cooking: 30–35 minutes**
**Level: 1**

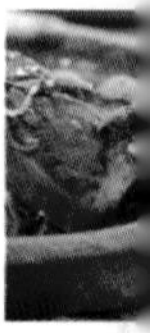

# PLUM PORK SPARERIBS

Place the spareribs in a large bowl and cover with the plum sauce. Cover with plastic wrap (cling film) and refrigerate for 1 hour. • Bring a large saucepan of salted water to a boil. • Add the rice and cook over medium heat for 10–15 minutes, until tender. • Drain well and set aside. • Place a grill pan over medium-high heat. • Brush the grill with the sesame oil. • Grill the spareribs for 5–6 minutes on each side, until cooked through. • Arrange a bed of the rice on individual serving plates and top with the spareribs. Garnish with the cilantro and serve hot.

**12 pork spareribs**

**2/3 cup (150 ml) Chinese plum sauce**

**1 1/2 cups (300 g) wild rice**

**3 tablespoons Asian sesame oil**

**3 tablespoons fresh cilantro (coriander) leaves**

**Serves: 4–6**
**Preparation: 5 minutes + 1 hour to marinate**
**Cooking: 20–27 minutes**
**Level: 1**

# PORK, BEAN, AND CABBAGE SALAD

Put the pork in a large bowl and cover with the 1/2 cup (125 ml) of the sweet chili sauce. Cover with plastic wrap (cling film) and refrigerate for 1 hour. • Preheat the oven to 350°F (180°C/gas 4). • Cook the green beans in a medium saucepan of boiling water for 2 minutes. • Drain and rinse under ice-cold water to stop the cooking process. Set aside. • Place a large nonstick frying pan over medium-high heat. • Cook the pork for 2 minutes on each side. • Transfer the pork to a large baking dish. • Bake for 15–20 minutes, until tender. • Remove from the oven and let rest for 5 minutes. Slice. • Cook the red cabbage with the remaining 1/4 cup (60 ml) of sweet chili sauce in a large frying pan over medium heat for 2 minutes, until slightly wilted. • Add the beans and cilantro. Toss well. • Serve the pork hot with the vegetables.

**1 pound (500 g) pork fillets**

**3/4 cup (180 ml) Thai sweet chili sauce**

**5 ounces (150 g) green beans**

**10 ounces (300 g) red cabbage, finely shredded**

**2 tablespoons fresh cilantro (coriander) leaves**

**Serves: 4**
**Preparation: 10 minutes + 1 hour to chill + 5 minutes to rest**
**Cooking: 18–20 minutes**
**Level: 1**

# LAMB CUTLETS WITH MINTED PEAS

Preheat the oven to 375°F (190°C/gas 5). • Fry the lamb in the oil from the marinated feta in a large frying pan over medium-high heat for 2 minutes on each side, until browned. • Transfer the lamb to a large baking dish. • Bake for 5–10 minutes, until tender. • Remove from the oven and let rest for 5 minutes. • Cook the peas in a small saucepan of boiling water for 1 minute, until cooked. • Mix the peas, feta, mint, and raspberry vinegar in a medium bowl and toss well. • Serve the lamb hot with the pea and feta salad.

**8 lamb cutlets, trimmed**

**5 ounces (150 g) marinated feta, oil reserved, cut into small cubes**

**1½ cups (185 g) frozen peas, thawed**

**3 tablespoons leaves fresh mint**

**3 tablespoons raspberry vinegar**

**Serves: 6–8**
**Preparation: 5 minutes + 5 minutes to rest**
**Cooking: 10–15 minutes**
**Level: 1**

# PESTO LAMB WITH NEW POTATOES

Place the lamb in a large bowl and cover with the pesto. Cover with plastic wrap (cling film) and chill for 1 hour. • Cook the potatoes in a large pot of boiling water for 15–20 minutes until tender. • Drain well and return to the pan. Add the butter and chives and toss well. • Cook the lamb in a nonstick frying pan over medium-high heat for 3–4 minutes on each side, until cooked through, but still slightly pink. • Slice the lamb thickly and serve hot with the potatoes.

- **4 lamb fillets, weighing about 6 ounces (180 g) each**
- **1/2 cup (125 ml) store-bought basil pesto**
- **1 1/4 pounds (550 g) new potatoes**
- **3 tablespoons butter, cut up**
- **2 tablespoons chopped chives**

**Serves: 4**
**Preparation: 10 minutes + 1 hour to chill**
**Cooking: 18–24 minutes**
**Level: 1**

# LAMB CUTLETS WITH BEET SALAD

Cook the beets in a medium saucepan of boiling water for 15–20 minutes, until tender. • Drain and let cool completely. • Peel the beets and cut in half. Set aside. • Cook the green beans in a medium saucepan of boiling water for 3 minutes until tender. • Drain and rinse under ice-cold water to stop the cooking process. • Arrange the beets and green beans on individual serving plates. • Season the lamb with salt. • Fry the lamb in the oil in a large frying pan over medium-high heat for 2–3 minutes on each side, until cooked. • Arrange the lamb cutlets on top of the vegetables. • Serve hot.

**6 baby beets (beetroot), trimmed**
**10 ounces (300 g) green beans**
**8 lamb cutlets, cut about 1/2 inch (1.5 cm) thick**
**Salt**
**3 tablespoons extra-virgin olive oil**

Serves: 4
Preparation: 15 minutes
Cooking: 22–29 minutes
Level: 1

# TAPENADE LAMB WITH MASHED EGGPLANT

Put the lamb in a large bowl and cover with the tapenade. Cover with plastic wrap (cling film) and refrigerate for 1 hour. • Preheat the oven to 400°F (200°C/gas 6). • Arrange the eggplants in a baking pan. • Roast for 20–30 minutes, turning often, until the skin has blackened and the insides are tender. • Remove from the oven and let cool completely. • Cut the eggplants in half and use a spoon to scoop out the flesh. Place in a large bowl and use a fork to mash until smooth. • Cook the potatoes in a large saucepan of boiling water for 5–7 minutes, until tender. • Drain and mash well. Mix the potatoes and tahini into the mashed eggplant. • Cook the lamb in a nonstick frying pan over medium-high heat for 3–4 minutes on each side, until cooked through, but still slightly pink. • Slice the lamb thickly and serve hot with the mashed eggplant.

**4 lamb fillets, weighing about 6 ounces (180 g) each**

**1/2 cup (125 ml) olive tapenade**

**4 large eggplants (aubergines)**

**10 ounces (300 g) potatoes, peeled and coarsely chopped**

**2 tablespoons tahini (sesame seed paste)**

**Serves: 4**
**Preparation: 10 minutes + 1 hour to marinate**
**Cooking: 28–41 minutes**
**Level: 1**

# COCONUT LAMB WITH RICE

Cook the lamb with the tomatoes in a large frying pan over medium heat for 2 minutes. • Pour in the coconut milk. • Cover and cook over low heat for 35–40 minutes until the lamb is tender. • Meanwhile, bring a large saucepan of salted water to a boil. • Add the rice and cook over medium heat for 10–15 minutes, until tender. • Drain well and set aside. • Add the cilantro to the lamb. • Serve hot on a bed of the rice.

- **1 3/4 pounds (800 g) lamb fillet (tenderloin), diced**
- **6 tomatoes, coarsely chopped**
- **2 cups (500 ml) coconut milk**
- **1 1/2 cups (300 g) basmati rice**
- **3 tablespoons fresh cilantro (coriander) leaves**

**Serves: 4**
**Preparation: 10 minutes**
**Cooking: 47–57 minutes**
**Level: 1**

# LAMB KLEFTIKO

Preheat the oven to 300°F (150°C/gas 2). • Put all the ingredients in a large baking dish. Cover with aluminum foil. • Bake for about 2 hours, until the lamb is tender. • Remove from the oven. Pour the liquid into a small saucepan. • Bring to a boil over high heat and cook until reduced by half. • Arrange the lamb and shallots in individual serving bowls. • Pour the cooking liquid into the bowls and serve hot.

**8 lamb chops, cut about 1/2 inch (1.5 cm) thick**
**12 shallots, unpeeled**
**2 cups (500 ml) dry white wine**
**Finely shredded zest and juice of 2 lemons**
**3 tablespoons fresh oregano leaves**

**Serves: 4**
**Preparation: 10 minutes**
**Cooking: 2 hours**
**Level: 1**

■ ■ ■ *In this classic Greek dish, the lamb is sealed in a baking dish and slowly baked until tender and succulent. There are many legends surrounding its invention. According to some, the Greeks learned to make it when they were fighting to free themselves from Ottoman rule. Hidden in the mountains, Greek soldiers would place all the ingredients in a dish and bury it over hot embers in the ground. No enticing food smells would emerge to let the enemy know their position.*

# LEMON LAMB WITH HALOUMI

Put the lamb in a large bowl. Add 1 tablespoon of the oil and the zest and juice of 1 lemon. • Cover with plastic wrap (cling film) and refrigerate for 1 hour. • Lift the lamb out of the marinade and fry in a large nonstick frying pan over medium-high heat for 2–3 minutes on each side, until cooked. • Remove from the pan and set aside. • Fry the cheese in 1 tablespoon of oil in a medium frying pan over high heat for 2 minutes on each side until browned. • Drain on paper towels. • Mix the arugula, fried haloumi, remaining 1 tablespoon of oil, and remaining lemon zest and juice in a medium bowl. • Toss well. Arrange the salad on individual serving plates and top with the lamb cutlets. • Serve hot.

**12 lamb cutlets, cut about 1/2 inch (1.5 cm) thick**

**3 tablespoons extra-virgin olive oil**

**Grated zest and juice of 2 lemons**

**8 ounces (250 g) haloumi or feta cheese, thickly sliced**

**3 cups (150 g) arugula (rocket) leaves**

**Serves: 4–6**
**Preparation: 10 minutes + 1 hour to chill**
**Cooking: 9–10 minutes**
**Level: 1**

# RED LAMB CURRY

Bring a large saucepan of salted water to a boil. • Add the rice and cook over medium heat for 10–15 minutes, until tender. • Drain well and set aside. • Place a wok over high heat. • When it is very hot, add the curry paste and lamb. Cook for 1 minute until aromatic. • Pour in the coconut milk and lime juice and bring to a boil. • Decrease the heat to low and cook for 5 minutes. • Serve the curry hot with the rice. Garnish with the lime wedges.

**$1^{1}/2$ cups (300 g) basmati rice**

**2 tablespoons Thai red curry paste**

**1 pound (500 g) lamb fillet (tenderloin), cut into bite-size pieces**

**$1^{2}/3$ cups (400 ml) coconut milk**

**1 tablespoon freshly squeezed lime juice, + lime wedges to serve**

Serves: 4
Preparation: 10 minutes
Cooking: 16–21 minutes
Level: 1

# LAMB KOFTE WITH MINTED COUSCOUS

Combine the lamb and bell pepper in a food processor and process until a coarse paste forms. • Use wet hands to shape the mixture into twelve sausage-shaped lengths. • Thread each kofte onto a metal skewer. • Mix the couscous and mint in a medium bowl. • Pour the stock over the couscous mixture. • Cover the bowl with plastic wrap (cling film) and let stand for 10 minutes, until the couscous has completely absorbed the liquid. • Fluff up the couscous with a fork and set aside. • Place a grill pan over high heat. • Grill the kofte for about 5 minutes on each side, until cooked through. • Serve hot on a bed of the minted couscous.

**$1^1/2$ pounds (750 g) ground (minced) lamb**
**1 red bell pepper (capsicum), seeded and finely chopped**
**2 cups (400 g) instant couscous**
**3 tablespoons finely chopped fresh mint**
**2 cups (500 ml) chicken stock, hot**

Serves: 4
Preparation: 15 minutes + 10 minutes to stand
Cooking: 10 minutes
Level: 1

# ROASTED HONEY MUSTARD LAMB

Put the lamb in a large bowl. Cover with the honey mustard and oil. • Cover with plastic wrap (cling film) and refrigerate for 1 hour. • Preheat the oven to 350°F (180°C/gas 4). • Arrange the lamb in a single layer in a large baking dish. • Bake for 25–30 minutes, or until tender. • Remove from the oven and let rest for 10 minutes. • Cook the parsnips in a large pot of boiling water for 8–10 minutes until tender. • Drain well and return to the pan. Add the crème fraîche and mash until smooth. • Slice the rack of lamb into four portions and serve hot with the mashed parsnip.

**3 pounds (1.5 kg) rack of lamb**

**1/2 cup (125 ml) honey mustard**

**1/3 cup (90 ml) extra-virgin olive oil**

**10 parsnips, peeled and diced**

**1/2 cup (125 ml) crème fraîche**

**Serves: 4**
**Preparation: 10 minutes + 1 hour to chill + 10 minutes to rest**
**Cooking: 33–40 minutes**
**Level: 1**

# LAMB AND WILD RICE SALAD

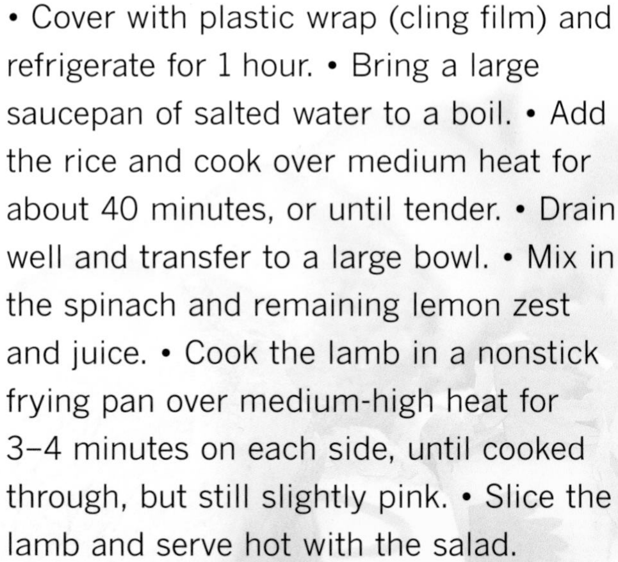

Put the lamb in a large bowl. Add the cumin and zest and juice of 1 lemon. • Cover with plastic wrap (cling film) and refrigerate for 1 hour. • Bring a large saucepan of salted water to a boil. • Add the rice and cook over medium heat for about 40 minutes, or until tender. • Drain well and transfer to a large bowl. • Mix in the spinach and remaining lemon zest and juice. • Cook the lamb in a nonstick frying pan over medium-high heat for 3–4 minutes on each side, until cooked through, but still slightly pink. • Slice the lamb and serve hot with the salad.

**1** **pound (500 g) lamb loin steaks, cut about 3/4 inch (2 cm) thick**

**1** **tablespoon ground cumin**

**Grated zest and juice of 2 lemons**

**1 1/2** **cups (300 g) wild rice**

**2** **cups (100 g) baby spinach leaves**

**Serves: 4**
**Preparation: 10 minutes + 1 hour to chill**
**Cooking: 46–48 minutes**
**Level: 1**

# FIVE-SPICE STEAK WITH WILTED SPINACH

Heat the oil in a large frying pan over medium-high heat. • Sprinkle the steaks with the five-spice powder. • Cook for 3–4 minutes on each side, depending on how well done you like your steak. • Remove from the heat. Cover and let rest for 5 minutes. • Cook the spinach in a medium saucepan of boiling water for 30 seconds until wilted. • Drain and return to the pan. Add the soy sauce and toss well. • Serve the steaks hot with the spinach.

**3 tablespoons Asian sesame oil**
**4 thick beef fillet steaks, about 6 ounces (180 g) each**
**2 tablespoons five-spice powder**
**10 ounces (300 g) baby spinach leaves**
**1/4 cup (60 ml) soy sauce**

Serves: 4
Preparation: 5 minutes
Cooking: 8 minutes + 5 minutes to rest
Level: 1

# BEEF RIB ROAST WITH CRISPY POTATOES

Preheat the oven to 400°F (200°C/ gas 6). • Sear the beef in 1/4 cup (60 ml) oil in a large frying pan over high heat for 2 minutes on each side until browned all over. • Transfer to a large roasting pan and season with salt and peppercorns. • Roast for about 25–35 minutes, depending on how well done you like your beef. • Remove from the oven and let rest for 10 minutes. • Meanwhile, cook the potatoes in a large pot of boiling water for 5 minutes. • Drain and toss to smash them slightly. • Pour the remaining 1/2 cup (125 ml) oil in a large roasting pan and heat in the oven for 10 minutes. • Add the potatoes and roast for about 30 minutes, until crispy. • Slice the rib roast into portions and serve hot with the potatoes.

**3 pounds (1.5 kg) standing rib roast (rib of beef), trimmed**

**3/4 cup (180 ml) extra-virgin olive oil**

**Salt**

**4 tablespoons green peppercorns**

**1 1/4 pounds (550 g) new potatoes, cut in half**

**Serves: 4**
**Preparation: 20 minutes + 10 minutes to rest**
**Cooking: 35–40 minutes**
**Level: 1**

# BALSAMIC STEAK WITH CARAMELIZED ONIONS

Cook the onions in 2 tablespoons of the oil in a large frying pan over very low heat for about 30 minutes, or until caramelized. • Meanwhile, heat the balsamic vinegar in a small saucepan over medium heat until it reduces by half. • Heat the remaining 2 tablespoons oil in a large frying pan over medium-high heat. • Cook the steaks for 3–4 minutes on each side, depending on how well done you like your steak. • Remove from the heat. Cover and let rest for 5 minutes. • Place the steaks on individual serving plates, topped with the onions and balsamic sauce with the arugula on the side.

- **6 onions, thinly sliced**
- **1/4 cup (60 ml) extra-virgin olive oil**
- **3/4 cup (180 ml) balsamic vinegar**
- **4 thick beef fillet steaks, about 6 ounces (180 g) each**
- **2 cups (100 g) arugula (rocket) leaves**

**Serves: 4**
**Preparation: 10 minutes + 5 minutes**
**Cooking: 40 minutes**
**Level: 1**

# BEEF VINDALOO

Combine the beef and vindaloo paste in a large nonstick frying pan over medium-high heat. • Cook for 1 minute until aromatic. • Add 1 tablespoon of stock to deglaze the pan and transfer the beef to a medium saucepan. • Add the onions and the remaining stock to the pan with the beef. Bring to a boil. • Decrease the heat to low, cover, and simmer for 1 hour, stirring occasionally. • Remove the lid and cook for about 30 minutes, or until the beef is very tender. • Meanwhile, bring a large saucepan of salted water to a boil. • Add the rice and cook over medium heat for 10–15 minutes, until tender. • Drain well. • Serve the vindaloo hot on a bed of the rice.

■ ■ ■ *Vindaloo is a spicy Indian dish made with meat or chicken flavored with a mixture of fiery spices. Vindaloo paste is available in Asian food stores, supermarkets, and from online food suppliers.*

- **1 3/4 pounds (800 g) beef chuck, cut into cubes**
- **2 tablespoons vindaloo paste**
- **1 cup (250 ml) beef stock**
- **2 onions, thinly sliced**
- **1 1/2 cups (300 g) basmati rice**

**Serves: 4**
**Preparation: 10 minutes**
**Cooking: 1 hour 30 minutes**
**Level: 2**

# BAKED SAUSAGES AND BEANS

Preheat the oven to 400°F (200°C/ gas 6). • Mix the tomatoes, cannellini beans, garlic, and oregano in a large baking dish. • Place a large nonstick frying pan over medium-high heat. • Cook the sausages, turning them occasionally, for about 5 minutes until browned. • Transfer the sausages to the baking dish. • Cover and bake for 15–20 minutes, until the sauce has thickened and the sausages are cooked through. • Serve hot.

**2 (14-ounce/800-g) cans chopped tomatoes, with juice**

**1 (14-ounce/400-g) can cannellini beans, drained**

**2 cloves garlic, finely chopped**

**2 tablespoons finely chopped fresh oregano**

**8 thick fresh beef sausages**

**Serves: 4–6**
**Preparation: 5 minutes**
**Cooking: 20–25 minutes**
**Level: 1**

# CHILI CON CARNE

Combine the ground beef, kidney beans, tomatoes, and chile peppers in a large saucepan. • Cook over medium heat for 20 minutes. • Decrease the heat to low and cook for 30 minutes. • Bring a large saucepan of salted water to a boil. • Add the rice and cook over medium heat for 10–15 minutes, until tender. • Drain well. • Serve the chili hot on a bed of the rice.

**1 pound (500 g) ground (minced) beef**

**1 (14-ounce/400-g) can red kidney beans, drained**

**2 (14-ounce/400-g) cans chopped tomatoes, with juice**

**4 large fresh red chile peppers, seeded and finely sliced**

**1½ cups (300 g) basmati rice**

**Serves: 4**
**Preparation: 5 minutes**
**Cooking: 60–65 minutes**
**Level: 1**

# BEEF CARPACCIO WITH GRAPEFRUIT SALAD

Wrap the beef tightly in plastic wrap (cling film) and freeze until firm, about 2 hours. • Mix the frisée, capers, and grapefruit in a medium bowl. Toss well and set aside. • Use a very sharp knife to cut the beef very thinly into 1/8-inch (3-mm) slices. • Lay the beef slices in a circle, slightly overlapping them and top with the salad. • Drizzle with the oil and serve at room temperature.

**1 3/4 pounds (800 g) best-quality beef fillet**

**2 cups (100 g) frisée**

**3/4 cup (90 g) capers**

**2 ruby grapefruit, cut into segments**

**1/4 cup (60 ml) extra-virgin olive oil**

**Serves: 4**
**Preparation: 20 minutes + 2 hours to freeze**
**Level: 1**

# BEEF STROGANOFF

Bring a large saucepan of salted water to a boil. • Add the rice and cook over medium heat for 10–15 minutes, until tender. • Drain well and set aside. • Cook the beef and mushrooms in a large nonstick frying pan over medium-high heat for 3 minutes. • Stir in the sour cream and thyme. • Decrease the heat to low and simmer for about 7 minutes, or until the beef and mushrooms are tender. • Serve the stroganoff hot with the rice and garnished with the extra sprigs of thyme.

**1½ cups (300 g) basmati rice**

**1 pound (500 g) beef fillet, cut into thin strips**

**1 pound (500 g) mushrooms, thinly sliced**

**1¼ cups (310 ml) sour cream**

**3 tablespoons finely chopped fresh thyme + sprigs to garnish**

Serves: 4
Preparation: 10 minutes
Cooking: 20–25 minutes
Level: 1

# SMOKY STEAK WITH TOMATO SALAD

Put the beef in a large bowl and cover with the marinade. Cover with plastic wrap (cling film) and refrigerate for 1 hour. • Place a grill pan over medium-high heat. • Cook the steaks for 4–5 minutes each, depending on how well done you like your steak. • Remove from the heat. Cover and let rest for 5 minutes. • Serve the steak hot, topped with the tomatoes, onion, and olives.

- **4 fillet beef steaks, about 6 ounces (180 g) each, cut about 3/4 inch (2 cm) thick**
- **3/4 cup (180 ml) smoky barbecue sauce**
- **6 tomatoes, thinly sliced**
- **1 red onion, thinly sliced**
- **1/2 cup (50 g) black olives, pitted**

**Serves: 4**
**Preparation: 10 minutes + 1 hour to chill + 5 minutes to stand**
**Cooking: 8–10 minutes**
**Level: 1**

# EGGS

# FRENCH TOAST WITH BACON AND MAPLE SYRUP

Dry-fry the bacon in a medium frying pan over medium heat for 5 minutes until crisp. • Set aside. • Melt the butter in a large frying pan. • Dip the bread slices into the eggs and cook over medium heat for 3 minutes on each side until golden. • Arrange the French toast on serving plates. Top with the bacon and drizzle with the maple syrup. • Serve hot.

**4 slices bacon, rind removed, if necessary**

**1/4 cup (60 g) butter, cut up**

**4 (3/4-inch/2-cm) slices sourdough bread**

**3 large eggs, lightly beaten**

**1/4 cup (60 ml) pure maple syrup**

Serves: 2
Preparation: 5 minutes
Cooking: 11 minutes
Level: 1

# POACHED EGGS ON TOAST

Preheat the oven to 350°F (180°C/gas 4). • Arrange the tomatoes in a baking pan and drizzle with the balsamic vinegar. • Roast for 6–8 minutes, until they begin to soften. • Bring a small saucepan of water to a boil. • Decrease the heat to low and use a spoon to create a whirlpool. • Crack the eggs, one at a time, into the center of the whirlpool. • Poach for about 3 minutes, or until the egg whites are slightly firm. • Use a slotted spoon to remove the eggs from the pan. Drain off any excess water. • Arrange the eggs on the toasted bread with the tomatoes on the side and garnished with the basil. • Serve hot.

**10 small vine-ripened tomatoes**
**1 tablespoon balsamic vinegar**
**4 large eggs**
**2 slices sourdough bread, toasted**
**8 fresh basil leaves**

**Serves: 2**
**Preparation: 5 minutes**
**Cooking: 9–11 minutes**
**Level: 1**

# BREAKFAST BURRITOS

Beat the eggs and cream in a large bowl. • Cook the egg mixture in a large nonstick frying pan over medium-low heat for about 5 minutes, stirring often, or until the eggs form large chunks. • Set aside and keep warm. • Warm the tortillas in a large frying pan over high heat, one at a time, until they begin to color. • Transfer to a flat surface and spread with the tomato salsa. • Top with the scrambled egg and watercress. • Fold the tortillas over and serve hot.

**8 large eggs**
**1 cup (250 ml) light (single) cream**
**4 flour tortillas**
**1/2 cup (125 ml) tomato salsa (or chutney)**
**2 cups (100 g) watercress**

**Serves: 4**
**Preparation: 5 minutes**
**Cooking: 7 minutes**
**Level: 1**

# SCRAMBLED EGGS WITH SMOKED SALMON

Beat the eggs and cream in a large bowl. • Melt the butter in a large frying pan over medium-low heat. • Add the egg mixture and cook for about 5 minutes, stirring often, or until the eggs form large chunks. • Serve the scrambled eggs hot with the smoked salmon and arugula.

- **8 large eggs**
- **1 cup (250 ml) light (single) cream**
- **1/4 cup (60 g) butter, cut up**
- **8 slices smoked salmon**
- **3 cups (150 g) arugula (rocket)**

**Serves: 4**
**Preparation: 5 minutes**
**Cooking: 5 minutes**
**Level: 1**

# ASIAN-STYLE SCRAMBLED EGGS

Beat the eggs and cream in a large bowl. • Cook the egg mixture in a large nonstick frying pan over medium-low heat for about 5 minutes, stirring often, until the eggs form large chunks. • Serve the scrambled eggs hot with the tomatoes, cilantro, and sweet chile sauce.

**8 large eggs**

**1 cup (250 ml) light (single) cream**

**4 large tomatoes, cut into small cubes**

**$1\frac{1}{2}$ cups (80 g) fresh cilantro (coriander) leaves**

**$\frac{1}{3}$ cup (90 ml) Thai sweet chili sauce**

**Serves: 4**
**Preparation: 5 minutes**
**Cooking: 5 minutes**
**Level: 1**

# EGG COCOTTE WITH LEEKS AND CHORIZO

Preheat the oven to 375°F (190°C/gas 5). • Grease four ramekins with 1 tablespoon of the butter. • Melt the remaining 2 tablespoons of butter in a large frying pan. • Add the chorizo and sauté for 3 minutes over medium heat. • Add the leeks and sauté for 3 minutes. • Pour in the cream and cook over low heat for about 2 minutes, or until the cream has thickened slightly. • Arrange the ramekins in a deep baking pan and pour in the mixture. • Break an egg into the center of each ramekin. • Fill the baking pan with boiling water to come halfway up the sides of the ramekins. • Bake for 15–18 minutes, until the eggs have set. • Serve hot.

■ ■ ■ *Cocotte comes from the French name for the ramekins in which this egg dish is cooked and served.*

**3 tablespoons butter**
**8 ounces (250 g) Spanish chorizo sausage, cut into small cubes**
**2 small leeks, trimmed and finely sliced**
**1/2 cup (125 ml) light (single) cream**
**4 large eggs**

**Serves: 4**
**Preparation: 10 minutes**
**Cooking: 23–28 minutes**
**Level: 1**

# EGG AND BAKED BEAN COCOTTE

Preheat the oven to 375°F (190°C/gas 5). • Arrange four ramekins in a deep baking pan. • Mix the cannellini beans, tomato purée, and parsley in a medium bowl. Season with pepper. • Spoon the bean mixture into the ramekins. • Break an egg into the center of each ramekin. • Fill the baking pan with boiling water to come halfway up the sides of the ramekins. • Bake for 15–18 minutes, until the eggs have set. • Serve hot.

**1 (14-ounce/400 g) can cannellini beans, drained**

**1²/3 cups (400 ml) tomato purée (passata)**

**2 tablespoons finely chopped fresh parsley**

**Freshly ground black pepper**

**4 large eggs**

Serves: 4
Preparation: 10 minutes
Cooking: 15–18 minutes
Level: 1

# SCOTCH EGGS

- $1^1/2$ pounds (750 g) sausage meat
- $1^1/4$ cups (310 ml) tomato salsa or chutney
- 8 hard-boiled eggs, shells removed
- $1^1/2$ cups (180 g) fine dry bread crumbs
- 1 quarts (1 liter) canola oil, for deep frying

Mix the sausage meat and $^1/_3$ cup (90 ml) of the tomato chutney in a large bowl. • Divide the sausage mixture into eight portions. Use your hands to form them into oval shapes. • Form the sausage mixture around the hard-cooked eggs. • Roll in the bread crumbs until well-coated. • Heat the oil in a large, deep frying pan. • Fry the eggs in batches for 5–7 minutes, until golden brown all over. • Drain on paper towels. • Serve hot or cold with the remaining tomato chutney.

Serves: 4–6
Preparation: 20 minutes
Cooking: 5–7 minutes per batch
Level: 2

# SPANISH TORTILLA

Heat 2 tablespoons of the oil in a large frying pan. • Add the potatoes and onions. Season with salt. • Cook, covered, over low heat for about 20 minutes, stirring often, or until the potatoes are tender. • Beat the eggs in a large bowl. • Remove the pan from the heat and add the potatoes and onions to the eggs. • Add the remaining 2 tablespoons oil to the pan. • Pour in the egg mixture and cook over medium heat for 1 minute. • Decrease the heat to low and cook for 10 minutes. • Slide a wooden spatula under the tortilla to loosen it from the pan. Turn the tortilla over. • Cook for 10 minutes more. • Cut into slices and serve hot or at room temperature.

**1/4 cup (60 ml) extra-virgin olive oil**

**2 pounds (1 kg) potatoes, peeled and very thinly sliced**

**2 red onions, thinly sliced**

**1/2 teaspoon salt**

**4 large eggs, lightly beaten**

Serves: 4
Preparation: 15 minutes
Cooking: 45 minutes
Level: 1

# BELL PEPPER AND BASIL OMELET

Preheat the oven to 350°F (180°C/gas 4). • Broil (grill) the bell peppers until the skins are blackened all over. • Wrap them in a paper bag for 5 minutes, then remove the skins and seeds. Slice into strips. • Heat the oil in a large ovenproof frying pan. • Add the bell peppers and basil. • Pour in the beaten eggs and season with salt. • Cook over medium-low heat for 5 minutes. • Bake for 20–25 minutes, until the eggs are set. • Cut into slices and serve hot.

**3 red bell peppers (capsicums)**
**3 tablespoons extra-virgin olive oil**
**4 tablespoons fresh basil leaves**
**8 large eggs, lightly beaten**
**1/2 teaspoon salt**

Serves: 4
Preparation: 25 minutes
Cooking: 35–40 minutes
Level: 1

# TOMATO SOUFFLÉ OMELET

Preheat the broiler (grill). • Beat the egg yolks and water in a medium bowl. • In a separate bowl, whisk the egg whites until soft peaks form. • Use a large rubber spatula to gently fold the beaten egg whites into the yolks. • Melt the butter in a medium frying pan. • Pour the egg mixture into the pan. Cook over medium heat for 1 minute. • Broil the omelet about 5 inches (12 cm) from the heat source for about 1 minute, or until golden. • Sprinkle with the tomato and onion. • Serve hot.

**3 large eggs, separated**
**1 tablespoon water**
**1 tablespoon butter**
**1 large tomato, finely chopped**
**1/2 red onion, finely sliced**

**Serves:** 2
**Preparation:** 10 minutes
**Cooking:** 2 minutes
**Level:** 1

# MINI CHEESE SOUFFLÉS



Preheat the oven to 325°F (170°C/gas 3). • Brush four individual soufflé dishes with 1 tablespoon of the butter. • Bring the milk to a boil in a small saucepan. • Melt the remaining butter in a medium saucepan. • Add the flour and cook over medium heat for 3 minutes. • Gradually pour in the hot milk, stirring constantly to prevent lumps from forming. • Cook over low heat for 10 minutes, stirring constantly. • Remove from the heat. • Beat the egg yolks in a small bowl. • Slowly add the Parmesan and beaten egg yolks to the milk mixture. • Let cool completely. • Beat the egg whites in a medium bowl until stiff peaks forms. • Use a large rubber spatula to fold the egg whites into the cheese mixture. • Pour the mixture into the prepared dishes until three-quarters full. • Arrange on a baking tray. • Bake for 25–30 minutes, until golden brown. • Serve hot.

**1/3 cup (90 g) butter**
**1 1/2 cups (375 ml) milk**
**1/3 cup (50 g) all-purpose (plain) flour**
**3 large eggs, separated**
**1 1/2 cups (180 g) freshly grated Parmesan cheese**

Serves: 4
Preparation: 10 minutes
Cooking: 40–45 minutes
Level: 2

# POACHED EGGS WITH ASPARAGUS SALAD

Blanch the asparagus in a large saucepan of boiling water for 2 minutes until tender. • Drain and rinse in ice-cold water to stop the cooking process. • Transfer to a large bowl. Add the arugula and 3 tablespoons of the vinegar and toss well. • Arrange the asparagus salad on four individual serving plates. • Bring a medium saucepan of water to a boil. • Add the remaining vinegar. Decrease the heat to low and use a spoon to create a whirlpool. • Crack the eggs, one at a time, into the center of the whirlpool. • Poach for about 3 minutes, or until the egg whites are slightly firm. • Use a slotted spoon to remove the eggs from the pan. Drain off any excess water. • Place the poached eggs on top of the salad. Season with pepper. • Serve at room temperature.

**1 pound (500 g) asparagus spears, wooden ends removed**

**4 cups (200 g) arugula (rocket)**

**1/3 cup (90 ml) red wine vinegar**

**8 large eggs**

**Freshly ground black pepper**

Serves: 4
Preparation: 5 minutes
Cooking: 5 minutes
Level: 1

# EGG AND VEGETABLE STIR-FRY

Pour the eggs into a large nonstick frying pan. • When the eggs have set on the bottom, slide a wooden spatula under the eggs to loosen them from the pan. Shake the pan with a rotating movement to spread. • Cook until nicely browned on the underside and the top is set. • Remove from the heat and slice into strips. Set aside. • Cook the kai-lan in a large saucepan of boiling water for 3 minutes. • Drain and rinse in ice-cold water to stop the cooking process. • Cook the mushrooms and quarter of a cup (60 ml) of hoisin sauce in a large frying pan over medium heat for 2 minutes. • Add the kai-lan, bean sprouts, and egg and cook for 2 minutes. • Add the remaining 1/4 cup (60 ml) hoisin sauce and toss well. • Serve hot.

**8 large eggs, lightly beaten**

**1 bunch kai-lan or Chinese broccoli, cut into short lengths**

**1 pound (500 g) button mushrooms, thinly sliced**

**1/2 cup (125 ml) hoisin sauce**

**3 ounces (90 g) bean sprouts**

Serves: 4
Preparation: 5 minutes
Cooking: 15 minutes
Level: 1

# ONE PAN BREAKFAST

Preheat the broiler (grill). • Fry the bacon and tomato in the oil in a small frying pan over medium heat for 2 minutes. • Add the spinach and mix well. • Crack in the eggs and cook over medium heat for 3 minutes. • Broil the eggs about 5 inches (12 cm) from the heat source for 2 minutes, or until the eggs are cooked to your liking. • Serve hot.

- **2 slices bacon, rind removed, if necessary**
- **1 tomato, finely chopped**
- **1 tablespoon extra-virgin olive oil**
- **1/2 cup (50 g) baby spinach leaves**
- **2 large eggs**

**Serves: 1**
**Preparation: 5 minutes**
**Cooking: 7 minutes**
**Level: 1**

■ ■ ■ *Packed with protein to provide energy throughout the day, eggs are the classic breakfast food. But eggs are also a good source of iron and sulfur, as well as vitamins A, B, D, and E. Eggs are relatively high in cholesterol and those following a low-cholesterol diet may wish to avoid or limit their consumption. There is some debate about whether eggs do constitute a health risk although most experts now agree that a moderate consumption of eggs does not appear to increase the risk of heart disease and stroke. It's always a good idea to check with your doctor on dietary issues. What is important to remember is that eggs should always be eaten cooked rather than raw. A tiny percentage of eggs are contaminated with harmful bacteria such as salmonella; cooking eggs entirely removes any danger from these bacteria.*

# POACHED EGGS ON POTATO GALETTE

Preheat the oven to 400°F (200°C/ gas 6). • Put the grated potatoes in a colander and squeeze out any excess moisture. • Heat 3 tablespoons of the butter in a large ovenproof frying pan and add half the potatoes. • Sprinkle with the Gruyère and cover with the remaining potatoes, pressing down firmly. • Cook over medium heat for 10 minutes until golden. • Turn out onto a plate and add the remaining butter to the pan. • Slide the galette back into the pan, crisp side up. • Bake for 10 minutes. • Bring a medium saucepan of water to a boil. • Decrease the heat to low and use a spoon to create a whirlpool. • Crack the eggs, one at a time, into the center of the whirlpool. • Poach for about 3 minutes, or until the egg whites are slightly firm. • Use a slotted spoon to remove the eggs from the pan. Drain off any excess water. • Cut the potato galette into quarters. • Top each quarter with 1/2 cup of arugula and a poached egg. • Serve hot.

**2 pounds (1 kg) potatoes, peeled and coarsely grated**
**1/3 cup (90 g) butter, cut up**
**1/2 cup (125 g) freshly grated Gruyère cheese**
**4 large eggs**
**2 cups (100 g) arugula (rocket)**

Serves: 4
Preparation: 15 minutes
Cooking: 25 minutes
Level: 1

# BOILED EGGS WITH SAUSAGE RAGOUT

Cook the onion and sausage in the oil in a large frying pan over low heat for 4 minutes. • Add the tomatoes. • Cook over medium heat for 10–15 minutes until thickened. • Remove from the heat, set aside, and keep warm. • Cook the eggs in a medium saucepan of barely simmering water for 7 minutes. • Drain well. • Place the eggs in eggcups and cut off the tops. • Serve the sausage ragout hot with the eggs.

- **1 large onion, finely chopped**
- **6 herbed pork sausages, coarsely chopped**
- **2 tablespoons extra-virgin olive oil**
- **$3^1/_4$ cups (810 g) peeled and chopped tomatoes, with juice**
- **8 large eggs**

**Serves: 4–6**
**Preparation: 10 minutes**
**Cooking: 21–24 minutes**
**Level: 1**

# MEXICAN EGGS

Fry the chile peppers in the oil in a large frying pan over medium heat for 1 minute until aromatic. • Add the tomatoes and red kidney beans. • Cook for 10 minutes until the tomatoes have softened. • Stir in the beaten eggs. • Cook for about 4 minutes, or until the eggs have set. • Serve hot.

**2 small bird's-eye chile peppers, seeded and finely chopped**

**2 tablespoons extra-virgin olive oil**

**4 tomatoes, finely chopped**

**1 (14-ounce/400 g) can red kidney beans, drained**

**8 eggs, lightly beaten**

**Serves: 4**
**Preparation: 5 minutes**
**Cooking: 15 minutes**
**Level: 1**

# QUICHE LORRAINE

Preheat the oven to 350°F (180°C/gas 4). • Line a 9-inch (23-cm) tart pan with a removable bottom with the pie pastry. Set aside. • Dry-fry the bacon in a medium frying pan over medium heat for 5 minutes until crispy. • Beat the eggs and cream in a large bowl. • Mix in the Cheddar and bacon. • Pour the filling into the tart shell. • Bake for 35–40 minutes until the filling has set and is golden. • Cut into slices and serve hot or at room temperature.

**1 sheet shortcrust pie pastry**

**6 slices bacon, thinly sliced and chopped into small pieces**

**6 large eggs**

**1 cup (250 ml) light (single) cream**

**1 cup (125 g) freshly grated Cheddar cheese**

Serves: 4
Preparation: 10 minutes
Cooking: 40–45 minutes
Level: 1

# BACON AND EGG MINI QUICHES

Preheat the oven to 300°F (150°C/gas 2). • Line four 4-inch (10-cm) tart pans with removable bottoms with the shortcrust pastry. • Refrigerate for 10 minutes. • Dry-fry the bacon in a medium frying pan over medium heat for 5 minutes until crispy. • Prick the pastry all over with a fork. • Bake for 10 minutes, or until lightly browned. • Increase the oven temperature to 350°F (180°C/gas 4). • Beat two of the eggs with the cream in a small bowl. • Put the bacon in the four tart shells. • Crack an egg into each case. • Pour in the cream mixture and season with pepper. • Bake for about 20 minutes, or until set. • Serve hot.

**2 sheets shortcrust pastry**

**4 slices bacon, rind removed, (if necessary), and cut in half**

**6 large eggs**

**1 cup (250 ml) heavy (double) cream**

**Freshly ground black pepper**

Serves: 4
Preparation: 20 minutes + 10 minutes to chill
Cooking: 35 minutes
Level: 1

# SPINACH AND BLUE CHEESE QUICHE

Preheat the oven to 350°F (180°C/gas 4). • Line a 9-inch (23-cm) tart pan with a removable bottom with the pie pastry. Set aside. • Cook the spinach in a small pan of lightly salted boiling water for 5 minutes, until tender. Drain well, squeeze out excess moisture, and chop coarsely with a large knife. • Beat the eggs and cream in a large bowl. • Mix in the spinach and blue cheese. • Pour the filling into the tart shell. • Bake for 35–40 minutes, until the filling has set and is golden. • Cut into slices and serve hot or at room temperature.

**1 sheet shortcrust pie pastry**
**8 ounces (250 g) spinach leaves, cooked and drained**
**6 large eggs**
**1 cup (250 ml) light (single) cream**
**1/2 cup (125 g) soft blue cheese**

Serves: 4
Preparation: 10 minutes
Cooking: 35–40 minutes
Level: 1

# SMOKED TROUT QUICHE

Preheat the oven to 350°F (180°C/gas 4). • Line a 9-inch (23-cm) tart pan with a removable bottom with the pie pastry. Set aside. • Beat the eggs and cream in a large bowl. • Mix in the trout and goat cheese. • Pour the filling into the tart shell. • Bake for 35–40 minutes, until the filling has set and is golden. • Cut into slices and serve hot or at room temperature.

- **1 sheet shortcrust pie pastry**
- **6 large eggs**
- **1 cup (250 ml) light (single) cream**
- **1/2 smoked trout, boned and flaked**
- **3/4 cup (180 g) marinated goat cheese or herbed chèvre**

**Serves: 4**
**Preparation: 10 minutes**
**Cooking: 35–40 minutes**
**Level: 1**

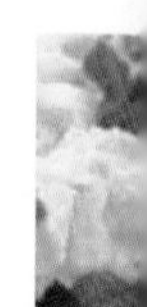

# EGG AND PROSCIUTTO PIZZAS

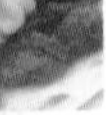

Preheat the oven to 400°F (200°C/ gas 6). • Put the tomatoes on a baking sheet. • Roast for 10 minutes, or until they begin to soften. • Spread the tomatoes over each pizza crust. • Lay four slices of prosciutto on each pizza. • Crack an egg into the center of each pizza. • Sprinkle with the goat cheese. • Bake for about 15 minutes, or until the crust is crisp and the eggs are cooked. • Serve hot.

**1 pound (500 g) cherry tomatoes**
**4 store-bought 8-inch (20-cm) pizza crusts**
**16 slices prosciutto (Parma ham)**
**4 large eggs**
**1 cup (250 g) crumbled soft goat cheese**

Serves: 4
Preparation: 10 minutes
Cooking: 25 minutes
Level: 1

# SPEEDY EGG PIZZA

Preheat the oven to 400°F (200°C/ gas 6). • Spread the tomato passata evenly over the pizza crust. • Sprinkle with the ham and mozzarella. • Crack an egg into each quarter of the pizza. • Bake for about 15 minutes, or until the crust is crispy and the eggs are cooked. • Serve hot.

**1/4 cup (60 ml) tomato purée (passata)**

**1 store-bought 12-inch (30-cm) pizza crust**

**2 cups (250 g) diced ham**

**1 1/2 cups (185 g) freshly grated mozzarella cheese**

**4 large eggs**

**Serves: 2–4**
**Preparation: 5 minutes**
**Cooking: 15 minutes**
**Level: 1**

# DESSERTS

# PEACH TARTE TATIN

Preheat the oven to 400°F (200°C/ gas 6). • Mix the peaches, butter, brown sugar, and vanilla seeds in a medium bowl. • Transfer the mixture to a medium nonstick ovenproof frying pan. • Cook over low heat for 15–20 minutes, until the peaches have softened. • Remove from the heat. • Place the puff pastry on top, cutting it to size, so that it sits on top of the peaches. • Bake for about 10 minutes, or until golden and slightly puffed. • Turn the tart out onto a cutting board. • Cut into portions and serve hot.

**4 peaches, pitted and cut in half**

**1 tablespoon butter, cut up**

**3 tablespoons brown sugar**

**Seeds from 1 vanilla pod**

**1 sheet puff pastry**

Serves: 4
Preparation: 10 minutes
Cooking: 25–30 minutes
Level: 2

# PEACHES WITH ALMOND CRUMBLE

Preheat the oven to 350°F (180°C/gas 4). • Mix the maple syrup and butter in a large baking pan. • Arrange the peaches cut-side down in the syrup. • Roast for 10 minutes until the peaches have softened. • Turn the peaches over so that the cut side is facing up. • Mix the amaretti and almonds in a small bowl. • Spoon the mixture over the peaches and drizzle with the syrup. • Bake for 10 minutes. • Serve hot.

**1/3 cup (90 ml) pure maple syrup**
**1 tablespoon butter, melted**
**4 peaches, cut in half and pitted**
**1 cup (125 g) crushed amaretti cookies**
**1 1/2 tablespoons flaked almonds**

**Serves: 4**
**Preparation: 10 minutes**
**Cooking: 20 minutes**
**Level: 1**

# GRILLED PEACHES WITH MINT YOGURT

Mix the yogurt and mint in a small bowl and refrigerate. • Dip the peach halves in the orange juice and sprinkle with the brown sugar. • Place a grill pan over medium-high heat. • Grill the peaches for 4 minutes on each side. • Serve the peaches warm with the mint yogurt.

- **3/4 cup (180 ml) plain yogurt**
- **2 tablespoons fresh mint leaves**
- **4 peaches, cut in half and pitted**
- **2 tablespoons freshly squeezed orange juice**
- **1/4 cup (50 g) firmly packed dark brown sugar**

**Serves: 4**
**Preparation: 10 minutes**
**Cooking: 8 minutes**
**Level: 1**

# GINGER POACHED PEARS

Combine the pears, water, superfine sugar, orange zest and juice, and ginger in a large saucepan. • Simmer over low heat for 30 minutes until the pears have just softened. • Remove the pears from the liquid and set aside. • Turn up the heat and boil for 10 minutes. • Return the pears to the liquid. • Serve warm.

**8 small pears, peeled**
**4 cups (1 liter) water**
**1 cup (200 g) superfine (caster) sugar**
**Juice and finely grated zest of 2 oranges**
**3 tablespoons candied or preserved ginger, finely sliced**

Serves: 4
Preparation: 10 minutes
Cooking: 40 minutes
Level: 1

# BAKED APPLES WITH MAPLE SYRUP

Preheat the oven to 350°F (180°C/gas 4). • Core the apples and lightly score the skin around the edge with a sharp knife. • Mix the dates and walnuts in a small bowl. • Stuff the mixture into the apples. • Arrange the apples in a baking pan. • Mix the maple syrup and water in a small bowl and pour over the apples. • Bake for about 50 minutes, or until the apples have softened. • Serve warm.

**4** **large apples**
**6** **pitted dates, finely chopped**
**1/2** **cup (50 g) finely chopped walnuts**
**1/2** **cup (125 ml) pure maple syrup**
**1/2** **cup (125 ml) water**

**Serves: 4**
**Preparation: 10 minutes**
**Cooking: 50 minutes**
**Level: 1**

# JAMAICAN BANANAS

Melt the butter with the brown sugar in a large frying pan over medium-low heat. • Peel the bananas and place them in the pan. • Cook for 2 minutes on each side. • Add the rum and cook for 2 minutes. • Serve warm with the ice cream on the side.

- **1/4 cup (60 g) butter, cut up**
- **1/2 cup (100 g) firmly packed dark brown sugar**
- **4 medium bananas**
- **1/4 cup (60 ml) rum**
- **4 scoops good-quality vanilla ice cream**

Serves: 2–4
Preparation: 5 minutes
Cooking: 8 minutes
Level: 1

# STUFFED FIGS

Preheat the oven to 375°F (190°C/gas 5). • Finely chop the orange zest and mix with the mascarpone and pecans in a small bowl. Set aside. • Remove the stems from the figs. • Use a sharp knife to make an opening in the figs. • Use a teaspoon to stuff the figs with the mascarpone mixture • Arrange the figs in a small baking dish. • Mix the orange juice and muscatel in a small bowl and pour over the figs. • Cover with aluminum foil. • Bake for 10 minutes. • Discard the foil and bake for about 10 minutes, or until softened. • Serve warm.

**Juice and zest of 1 orange**

**3/4 cup (180 ml) fresh mascarpone cheese**

**3/4 cup (75 g) coarsely chopped pecans**

**12 dried figs**

**3/4 cup (180 ml) sweet muscatel wine**

Serves: 4–6
Preparation: 10 minutes
Cooking: 20 minutes
Level: 1

# GOOEY CHOCOLATE PUDDING

Preheat the oven to 400°F (200°C/ gas 6). • Grease four small ramekins with 1 tablespoon of the butter and sprinkle with the superfine sugar, shaking out the excess. • Melt the chocolate and remaining 7 tablespoons butter in a double boiler over barely simmering water. • Set aside. • Beat the eggs, egg yolks, and remaining superfine sugar in a large bowl with an electric mixer at high speed until pale and thick. • Use a large rubber spatula to fold the chocolate mixture and flour into the beaten eggs. • Pour the mixture evenly into the prepared ramekins. • Bake for about 10 minutes, or until set. • Serve warm.

**1/2 cup (125 g) butter, cut up**

**1/2 cup (100 g) superfine (caster) sugar**

**4 ounces (125 g) semisweet or dark chocolate, coarsely chopped**

**2 large eggs and 2 large egg yolks**

**2 teaspoons all-purpose (plain) flour**

**Serves: 4**
**Preparation: 15 minutes**
**Cooking: 10 minutes**
**Level: 1**

# WHITE CHOCOLATE PARFAIT

Line a 9 x 5-inch (23 x 18-cm) terrine mold or loaf pan with plastic wrap (cling film). • Melt the white chocolate in a double boiler over barely simmering water. • Set aside. • Beat the egg yolks in a large bowl with an electric mixer at high speed until pale and thick. • Mix the superfine sugar and water in a small saucepan over medium heat, stirring often, until the sugar has dissolved. Bring to a boil. • Decrease the heat to low and simmer for 3 minutes. • With the mixer at low speed, gradually beat the syrup into the beaten egg yolks. Beat until the mixture has cooled. Stir in the chocolate. • Use a large rubber spatula to fold in the whipped cream. • Pour the mixture into the prepared mold. • Cover with plastic wrap and freeze overnight. • Cut into slices and serve.

**6 ounces (180 g) white chocolate, coarsely chopped**
**5 large egg yolks**
**1/2 cup (100 g) superfine (caster) sugar**
**1/4 cup (60 ml) water**
**1 2/3 cups (400 ml) whipped cream**

**Serves: 4–6**
**Preparation: 20 minutes + overnight to freeze**
**Cooking: 3 minutes**
**Level: 1**

# CHOCOLATE AND HAZELNUT POTS

Melt the chocolate in a double boiler over barely simmering water. • Transfer to a large bowl and let cool slightly. • Use a large rubber spatula to mix the cream, hazelnuts, and vanilla into the melted chocolate. • Pour the mixture evenly into four serving dishes. • Cover with plastic wrap (cling film) and chill for 15 minutes. • Serve with the sliced strawberries.

- **4 ounces (125 g) semisweet or dark chocolate**
- **3/4 cup (180 ml) heavy (double) cream**
- **1/2 cup (50 g) roasted and coarsely chopped hazelnuts**
- **1 teaspoon vanilla extract (essence)**
- **1 cup (250 g) fresh strawberries, sliced**

**Serves: 4**
**Preparation: 10 minutes + 15 minutes to chill**
**Level: 1**

# STRAWBERRY FROZEN YOGURT

Process the strawberries, confectioners' sugar, and lemon juice in a food processor until smooth. • Transfer the mixture into a large bowl. • Stir in the yogurt and whipped cream until well mixed. • If you have an ice-cream machine, pour the mixture into it and follow the instructions. • If you don't have an ice-cream machine, freeze the mixture for 9 hours, stirring well every 3 hours. • Scoop into bowls to serve.

**1 cup (250 g) strawberries, hulled**
**2/3 cup (100 g) confectioners' (icing) sugar**
**1/3 cup (90 ml) freshly squeezed lemon juice**
**1 cup (250 ml) plain yogurt**
**2/3 cup (150 ml) whipped cream**

**Serves: 4**
**Preparation: 15 minutes + time to freeze**
**Level: 1**

# VANILLA ICE CREAM

Bring the milk, cream, and vanilla seeds to a boil in a medium saucepan. • Remove from the heat and let cool slightly. • Beat the egg yolks and superfine sugar in a double boiler until well blended. • Gradually pour in the warm milk mixture. • Cook over low heat, stirring constantly with a wooden spoon, until the mixture lightly coats a metal spoon or registers 160°F (71°C) on an instant-read thermometer. • Immediately plunge the pan into a bowl of ice water and stir until cooled. • If you have an ice-cream machine, pour the mixture into it and follow the instructions. • If you don't have an ice-cream machine, freeze the mixture for 9 hours, stirring well every 3 hours. • Scoop into bowls to serve.

**2 cups (500 ml) milk**

**1 cup (250 ml) light (single) cream**

**Seeds from 1 vanilla pod**

**4 large egg yolks**

**3/4 cup (150 g) superfine (caster) sugar**

Serves: 4
Preparation: 15 minutes + time to freeze
Cooking: 10 minutes
Level: 1

# CHOCOLATE MINT SORBET

Bring the water and superfine sugar to a boil in a medium saucepan. • Decrease the heat to low and simmer until the sugar has dissolved. • Stir in the cocoa powder and mint. Simmer for 15 minutes. • Remove from the heat and let cool completely. • If you have an ice-cream machine, pour the mixture into it and follow the instructions. • If you don't have an ice-cream machine, freeze the mixture for 9 hours, stirring well every 3 hours. • Scoop into bowls and serve with the wafers.

**2¾ cups (680 ml) water**

**1 cup (200 g) superfine (caster) sugar**

**1 cup (150 g) unsweetened cocoa powder**

**4 sprigs fresh mint, finely chopped**

**Ice cream wafers or other thin, crisp cookies, to serve**

Serves: 4
Preparation: 20 minutes + time to freeze
Cooking: 20 minutes
Level: 1

# BLUEBERRY AND MASCARPONE ICE CREAM

Bring the water and superfine sugar to a boil in a medium saucepan. • Decrease the heat to low and simmer until the sugar has dissolved. • Remove from the heat. Stir in the blueberries and let cool completely. • Mix in the mascarpone and cream. • If you have an ice-cream machine, pour the mixture into it and follow the instructions. If you don't have an ice-cream machine, freeze the mixture for 9 hours, stirring well every 3 hours.• Scoop into bowls to serve.

**1$^{3}/_{4}$ cups (430 ml) water**

**1$^{1}/_{2}$ cups (300 g) superfine (caster) sugar**

**$^{1}/_{2}$ cup (125 g) blueberries**

**2 cups (500 ml) fresh mascarpone cheese**

**$^{1}/_{2}$ cup (125 ml) heavy (double) cream**

Serves: 4
Preparation: 15 minutes + time to freeze
Cooking: 5 minutes
Level: 1

# ESPRESSO GRANITA

Combine the superfine sugar and cocoa powder in a large saucepan. Slowly mix in the water until smooth. • Bring to a boil, stirring often, until the sugar has dissolved. • Decrease the heat to low and simmer for 3 minutes. • Remove from the heat and stir in the coffee. • Pour the mixture into a freezeproof container and let cool completely. • Freeze for 2 hours until partly set. • Remove and stir with a fork to break up the ice crystals. • Return to the freezer and freeze for 2 hours. • Stir again to break up the ice crystals. • Serve in espresso cups, with the whipped cream on the side if liked.

**1 cup (200 g) superfine (caster) sugar**

**1½ tablespoons unsweetened cocoa powder**

**½ cup (125 ml) water**

**5 cups (1.25 liters) very strong brewed coffee**

**1 cup (250 ml) whipped cream (optional)**

Serves: 4
Preparation: 20 minutes + 4 hours to freeze
Cooking: 5 minutes
Level: 1

# BLOOD ORANGE TART

Preheat the oven to 350°F (180°C/gas 4). • Line a 10-inch (25-cm) tart pan with a removable bottom with the pastry. • Prick all over with a fork. • Bake for 15 minutes. • Reduce the oven temperature to 300°F (150°C/gas 2). • Mix the eggs, superfine sugar, and cream in a medium bowl. Remove the zest from one of the oranges and cut the flesh into thin slices. Squeeze the juice from the remaining orange. • Stir the juice into the beaten egg mixture. • Pour the mixture into pastry shell and arrange the orange slices on top of the filling. • Bake for 25–30 minutes, until the filling has set. • Let cool completely before serving.

**1 sheet shortcrust pie pastry**
**4 large eggs**
**1 cup (200 g) superfine (caster) sugar**
**1 cup (250 ml) light (single) cream**
**2 blood oranges**

**Serves: 6–8**
**Preparation: 10 minutes + cooling time**
**Cooking: 40–45 minutes**
**Level: 1**

# CHOCOLATE AND RASPBERRY TART

Preheat the oven to 350°F (180°C/gas 4). • Line a 10-inch (25-cm) tart pan with a removable bottom with the pastry. • Prick all over with a fork. • Bake for 15 minutes. • Reduce the oven temperature to 300°F (150°C/gas 2). • Melt the chocolate with the cream in a double boiler over barely simmering water. • Transfer to a large bowl. • With an electric mixer at high speed, beat in the egg yolks. • Use a large rubber spatula to fold in the raspberries. • Pour the mixture into pastry shell. • Bake for 25–30 minutes, until the filling has set. • Let cool completely and serve.

**1 sheet shortcrust pie pastry**
**10 ounces (300 g) semisweet or dark chocolate**
**2 cups (500 ml) light (single) cream**
**4 large egg yolks**
**1 cup (250 g) fresh raspberries**

**Serves: 6–8**
**Preparation: 10 minutes**
**Cooking: 40–45 minutes**
**Level: 1**

# PORTUGUESE-STYLE CRÈME CARAMEL

Preheat the oven to 350°F (180°C/gas 4). • Combine the brown sugar and water in a small saucepan. Stir over low heat until the sugar dissolves. • Turn up the heat to medium and bring to a boil. • Cook for about 6 minutes, or until the syrup thickens. • Pour the syrup into an 8-inch (20-cm) round springform pan. • With an electric mixer at high speed, beat the eggs and egg yolks and superfine sugar in a large bowl until pale and creamy. • Bring the milk to a boil in a medium saucepan. • Gradually whisk the hot milk into the egg mixture. • Pour the mixture into the springform pan. • Place in a large roasting pan. Pour boiling water into the roasting pan to come halfway up the sides of the springform pan. • Bake for about 1 hour, or until the custard has set. • Let the custard cool completely in the waterbath. • Chill overnight. • Gently run a knife around the edge of the custard. Turn out onto a plate and serve.

- **1/2 cup (100 g) firmly packed dark brown sugar**
- **1 tablespoon water**
- **6 large eggs and 6 large egg yolks**
- **2 1/3 cups (470 g) superfine (caster) sugar**
- **3 2/3 cups (900 ml) milk**

Serves: 6
Preparation: 10 minutes + overnight to chill
Cooking: 70 minutes
Level: 2

# SWEET BAKED RICOTTA

Preheat the oven to 325°F (170°C/gas 3). • Mix the ricotta, marmalade, eggs, brandy, and flour in a large bowl. • Spoon the mixture evenly into individual serving-size ramekins each with a capacity of about 1 cup (250 ml). • Bake for 40 minutes. • Turn off the oven and leave the door ajar until the ricotta is completely cool. • Serve at room temperature.

- **2¼ cups (600 g) fresh ricotta cheese, drained**
- **⅓ cup (90 g) orange marmalade**
- **2 large eggs, lightly beaten**
- **2 tablespoons (30 ml) brandy**
- **2 tablespoons all-purpose (plain) flour**

**Serves: 4**
**Preparation: 10 minutes**
**Cooking: 40 minutes**
**Level: 1**

# VANILLA PANNA COTTA

Mix the cream, superfine sugar, and vanilla seeds in a medium saucepan. • Bring to a boil and simmer over low heat for 2 minutes. • Remove from the heat. • Stir in the gelatin mixture until completely dissolved. • Spoon the mixture evenly into four 7-ounce (200-g) custard cups, ramekins, or dariole molds. • Chill for 6 hours, until set. • Turn the panna cotta out onto serving plates. • Serve with fresh strawberries.

**2 cups (500 ml) light (single) cream**

**1/2 cup (100 g) superfine (caster) sugar**

**Seeds of 1 vanilla pod**

**2 teaspoons plain gelatin, soaked in 2 tablespoons cold water until softened**

**1 cup (250 g) strawberries, hulled**

Serves: 4
Preparation: 15 minutes + 6 hours to chill
Cooking: 5 minutes
Level: 1

# BLACKBERRY FOOL

Process the blackberries with 1 tablespoon of the confectioners' sugar and the lemon juice in a food processor until smooth. • With an electric mixer at high speed, beat the cream and the remaining 3 tablespoons of confectioners' sugar in a medium bowl until stiff. • Use a large rubber spatula to fold in the yogurt and half the blackberry purée. • Spoon one-third of the blackberry purée evenly into four serving glasses. • Top with half of the cream. Repeat in layers until the glasses are filled. • Serve immediately.

- **2 cups (500 g) blackberries**
- **1/4 cup (30 g) confectioners' (icing) sugar**
- **2 teaspoons freshly squeezed lemon juice**
- **1 cup (250 ml) light (single) cream**
- **1/2 cup (125 ml) plain yogurt**

**Serves: 4**
**Preparation: 15 minutes**
**Level: 1**

■ ■ ■ *A fool is a traditional British dessert made by folding raw or cooked puréed fruit into whipped cream. The name is thought to derive from the French word* fouler *(to mash). Any fruit can be used, but berries and rhubarb work particularly well.*

# CARAMELIZED RUBY GRAPEFRUIT

Cut the grapefruits into 3/4-inch (2-cm) slices and set aside. • Combine the brown sugar, water, and vanilla seeds in a large frying pan over low heat and simmer until the sugar has dissolved. • Turn up the heat and simmer over medium heat for 10 minutes, until thickened. • Add the grapefruit slices and simmer for 2 minutes on each side. • Serve the grapefruit warm with the yogurt.

**4 ruby grapefruits, peeled and zest removed**

**1 cup (200 g) firmly packed light brown sugar**

**1 cup (250 ml) water**

**Seeds of 1 vanilla pod**

**3/4 cup (180 ml) vanilla-flavored yogurt**

**Serves: 4**
**Preparation: 15 minutes**
**Cooking: 15 minutes**
**Level: 1**

# MELON AND CILANTRO SALAD

Slice the melons in half. • Remove the skins and seeds and slice into bite-sized cubes. • Combine the melons in a large bowl. Add the cilantro and almonds. • Toss well and serve.

- **1/4 rock melon**
- **1/4 honeydew melon**
- **1/4 small watermelon**
- **3 tablespoons coarsely chopped cilantro (coriander)**
- **1/4 cup (40 g) flaked almonds, toasted**

**Serves: 4**
**Preparation: 15 minutes**
**Level: 1**

# SUMMER FRUIT COMPOTE

Preheat the oven to 350°F (180°C/gas 4). • Combine the peaches, apricots, plums, and blueberries in a large baking dish and sprinkle with the superfine sugar. • Bake for 25–30 minutes until the fruit has softened. • Remove from the oven and let cool completely. • Chill for 1 hour and serve.

- **3 peaches, cut in half and pitted (stoned)**
- **6 apricots, cut in half and pitted (stoned)**
- **6 plums, cut in half and pitted (stoned)**
- **1 cup (250 g) blueberries**
- **1/4 cup (50 g) superfine (caster) sugar**

**Serves: 4**
**Preparation: 10 minutes + 1 hour to chill**
**Cooking: 25–30 minutes**
**Level: 1**

# STRAWBERRY JELLIES

Heat half the rosé wine and the superfine sugar in a medium saucepan until the sugar has dissolved. • Remove from the heat. • Stir in the gelatin mixture until completely dissolved. • Add the remaining wine and lime juice and let cool completely. • Arrange the strawberries in four individual terrine or other molds each with a capacity of about 1 cup (250 ml). • Reserve 2/3 cup (150 ml) of the gelatin mixture and pour the remaining mixture into the molds. • Cover with plastic wrap (cling film) and top with a plate. • Chill for 1 hour. • Warm the remaining gelatin mixture and pour it over the jelly. • Cover with plastic wrap and chill overnight. • Dip the molds into hot water and turn out onto individual serving plates. • Serve immediately.

**1 3/4 cups (430 ml) sparkling rosé wine**
**1/4 cup (50 g) superfine (caster) sugar**
**2 teaspoons plain gelatin, soaked in 2 tablespoons cold water until softened**
**1 tablespoon freshly squeezed lime juice**
**2 3/4 cups (680 g) strawberries, hulled and cut in half**

**Serves: 4**
**Preparation: 1 hour 15 minutes + overnight to chill**
**Cooking: 5 minutes**
**Level: 2**

# CHERRY BRÛLÉE

Spread the cherries evenly in a shallow ovenproof baking dish about 9 inches (23 cm) square). • Bring the light and heavy cream to a boil in a small saucepan. • Remove from the heat. • With an electric mixer at high speed, beat the egg yolks and 2 tablespoons of the superfine sugar in a large bowl until pale and thick. • Gradually pour in the hot cream, mixing well. • Return the mixture to the saucepan and whisk over low heat for 5 minutes, until thickened. Do not let it boil. • Remove from the heat and let cool slightly. • Pour the mixture over the cherries. • Chill for 4 hours. • Preheat a broiler (grill). • Sprinkle the remaining 2 tablespoons of superfine sugar over the custard. • Broil the custard about 5 inches (12 cm) from the heat source for about 5 minutes, or until browned. • Serve immediately.

**2 cups (500 g) fresh cherries, pitted (stoned)**

**1/2 cup (125 ml) light (single) cream**

**1/2 cup (125 ml) heavy (double) cream**

**2 large egg yolks**

**1/4 cup (50 g) superfine (caster) sugar**

Serves: 4
Preparation: 25 minutes + 4 hours to chill
Cooking: 15 minutes
Level: 1

# MINI PASSIONFRUIT SOUFFLÉS

Preheat the oven to 425°F (220°C/gas 7). • Butter four 1-cup (250-cm) soufflé dishes and sprinkle evenly with the confectioners' sugar, shaking out the excess. • With an electric mixer at high speed, beat the egg yolks, passionfruit pulp, lemon juice, and half the remaining confectioners' sugar in a large bowl until well combined. • With mixer at high speed, beat the egg whites and the remaining confectioners' sugar in a large bowl until stiff peaks form. • Use a large rubber spatula to fold the egg whites into the passionfruit mixture. • Spoon the mixture into the prepared dishes and bang them once on the work surface to remove any air bubbles. • Bake for 20–25 minutes or until well risen. • Serve immediately.

- **2/3 cup (100 g) confectioners' (icing) sugar**
- **2 large egg yolks**
- **1/2 cup (125 g) passionfruit pulp**
- **2 tablespoons freshly squeezed lemon juice**
- **6 large egg whites**

**Serves: 4**
**Preparation: 20 minutes**
**Cooking: 20–25 minutes**
**Level: 1**

# BLUEBERRY MERINGUES

Preheat the oven to 300°F (150°C/gas 2). • Line two baking sheets with parchment (baking) paper and mark four 3-inch (8-cm) circles on the paper. • Beat the egg whites in a large bowl with an electric mixer at medium speed until frothy. • With mixer at high speed, gradually add the superfine sugar, beating until stiff, glossy peaks form. • Spread the mixture into rounds on the prepared sheets. • Bake for 40–45 minutes until crisp. • Turn off the oven and leave the door ajar until the meringues are completely cool. • Carefully remove the paper. • Mix the blueberries and hazelnut liqueur in a small bowl. • Stir in the cream. • Sandwich the meringues together in pairs with the blueberry liqueur cream and serve immediately.

- **4 large egg whites**
- **1 cup (250 g) superfine (caster) sugar**
- **1 1/2 cups (375 g) blueberries**
- **2 tablespoons hazelnut liqueur**
- **2 cups (500 ml) whipped cream**

**Serves: 4**
**Preparation: 25 minutes + cooling time**
**Cooking: 40–45 minutes**
**Level: 1**

# BAKED FRUIT MERINGUES

Preheat the oven to 425°F (220°C/gas 7). • Beat the egg whites in a large bowl with an electric mixer at medium speed until frothy. • With mixer at high speed, gradually beat in the superfine sugar, beating until stiff, glossy peaks form. • Mix the strawberries, blackberries, and almonds in a medium bowl. • Spoon the fruit mixture evenly into four 1-cup (250 ml) ramekins. • Top each one with a dollop of the meringue. • Bake for 7–10 minutes until lightly browned. • Serve warm.

- **2 large egg whites**
- **1/2 cup (100 g) superfine (caster) sugar**
- **1 1/2 cups (375 g) strawberries, hulled**
- **1 1/2 cups (375 g) blackberries**
- **1/3 cup (50 g) ground almonds**

**Serves: 4**
**Preparation: 10 minutes**
**Cooking: 7–10 minutes**
**Level: 1**

# APPLE STRUDEL

Preheat the oven to 425°F (220°C/gas 7). • Cook the apples in 2 tablespoons of the butter in a medium saucepan over medium heat for 3 minutes. • Add the golden raisins and almonds. Cook for 3 minutes. • Remove from the heat, drain off any excess liquid, and set aside. • Melt the remaining 2 tablespoons of butter in a small saucepan. • Butter a large baking sheet. • Place one sheet of phyllo pastry on the prepared baking sheet. • Brush the top of the phyllo sheet with melted butter. Cover with another phyllo sheet. Repeat with all the phyllo sheets. • Spread the apple mixture on one side of the phyllo. • Fold the pastry over, sealing the edges with the melted butter. • Brush the top with the melted butter. • Bake for 20–25 minutes, until golden. • Cut into slices and serve warm.

**3 tart apples, peeled, cored, and thinly sliced**

**1/4 cup (60 g) butter, cut up**

**1/4 cup (45 g) golden raisins (sultanas)**

**1/3 cup (50 g) ground almonds**

**6 sheets frozen phyllo (filo) pastry, thawed**

Serves: 4
Preparation: 25 minutes
Cooking: 26–31 minutes
Level: 1

# APPLE TURNOVERS

Preheat the oven to 400°F (200°C/ gas 6). • Cut the pastry into four squares. • Place an apple quarter in the center of each pastry square. • Draw up the pastry edges and pinch them together to seal. • Arrange the turnovers on a baking sheet. • Bake for 15–20 minutes until golden. • Mix the water and corn syrup and drizzle over the turnovers. • Serve hot with a scoop of ice cream.

- **1 sheet puff pastry**
- **1 apple, peeled, cored, and cut into quarters**
- **1/2 cup (125 ml) hot water**
- **1/4 cup (60 ml) light corn syrup or golden syrup**
- **4 scoops good-quality vanilla ice cream**

**Serves: 4**
**Preparation: 10 minutes**
**Cooking: 15–20 minutes**
**Level: 1**

# WAFFLES WITH BAKED PLUMS

Preheat the oven to 350°F (180°C/gas 4). • Place the plums, cut-side down, on a small baking sheet. • Bake for 10 minutes. • Turn them over and bake for 5 minutes. • Heat the waffles in the oven for 5 minutes. • Place the waffles on individual serving plates. • Arrange the plum halves on top and drizzle with the maple syrup. Dust with the confectioners' sugar. • Serve warm with the ice cream on the side.

- **4 plums, cut in half and pitted (stoned)**
- **4 frozen waffles**
- **1/2 cup (125 ml) pure maple syrup**
- **2 tablespoons confectioners' (icing) sugar**
- **4 scoops good-quality vanilla ice cream**

**Serves: 2–4**
**Preparation: 10 minutes**
**Cooking: 20 minutes**
**Level: 1**

# INDIVIDUAL BREAD AND BUTTER PUDDINGS

Preheat the oven to 325°F (170°C/gas 3). • With an electric mixer at high speed, beat the eggs and superfine sugar in a large bowl until pale and creamy. • Bring the milk to a boil in a medium saucepan. • Gradually whisk the hot milk into the egg mixture. • Butter the bread and cut into triangles. • Place the bread in four 1-cup (250-ml) ramekins and pour in the custard mixture. • Place the ramekins in a baking dish. Pour boiling water into the baking dish to come halfway up the sides of the ramekins. • Bake for 25–30 minutes until set. • Preheat a broiler (grill). Broil the puddings about 5 inches (12 cm) from the heat source for about 5 minutes, or until browned. • Serve immediately.

■ ■ ■ *Fruit danishes or croissants can be used as an alternative to bread.*

**3 large eggs**
**1/4 cup (50 g) superfine (caster) sugar**
**1 1/2 cups (375 ml) milk**
**1/4 cup (60 g) butter, cut up**
**12 slices cinnamon raisin bread**

**Serves: 4**
**Preparation: 15 minutes**
**Cooking: 35–40 minutes**
**Level: 1**

# BRANDY SNAPS

- 1/2 cup (125 g) butter, cut up
- 1 cup (200 g) firmly packed dark brown sugar
- 1/2 cup (125 ml) light corn syrup or golden syrup
- 3/4 cup (125 g) all-purpose (plain) flour
- 2 cups (500 ml) heavy (double) cream

Serves: 4–6
Preparation: 25 minutes
Cooking: 8–10 minutes per batch
Level: 1

Preheat the oven to 325°F (170°C/gas 3). • Line two cookie sheets with parchment (baking) paper. • Butter two rolling pins. • Melt the butter with the brown sugar and corn syrup in a small saucepan over low heat, stirring constantly until the sugar has dissolved. • Remove from the heat and let cool completely. • Mix in the flour. Drop teaspoons of the mixture 2 inches (5 cm) apart onto the prepared sheets. • Bake for 8–10 minutes until golden brown. • Working quickly, use a spatula to lift each cookie from the sheet and drape it over a rolling pin. • Slide each cookie off the pin onto a rack to finish cooling. • If the cookies harden too quickly, return the cookie sheets to the oven for 1–2 minutes, or until the cookies are soft again. • Beat the cream in a medium bowl until stiff. • Spoon the cream into a pastry bag fitted with a small plain tip. • Fill the brandy snaps with the cream and serve immediately.

# INDEX